WALKING IN THE SPIRIT

BY ALISON CHANT

Walking in the Spirit

By

Alison Chant

Copyright © Alison Chant 2008

ISBN 1-931178-09-7

All rights in this book are reserved. No part of this book may be reproduced in any manner whatsoever without the written permission of the author except brief quotations embodied in critical articles or reviews.

All Bible quotes in this book come from The New International Version unless otherwise stated.

FOR ORDERING INFORMATION, PLEASE CONATCT:

VISION PUBLISHING

1115 D STREET, RAMONA CALIFORNIA 92065

www.visionpublishingservices.com

1-800-9-VISION

Vision International College
PO Box 84, Macquarie Fields
NSW 2564, Australia
Ph 02 9829 1340
Fx 02 9829 1420
visioncc@bigpond.net.au

TABLE OF CONTENTS

Foreword 5

Preface 6

Ch. 1 How we Should Live 9

Ch. 2 How we Should Pray... 19

Ch. 3 Gaining Character... 27

Ch. 4 Pleasing God 37

Ch. 5 Living by the Spirit.. 49

Ch. 6 The Battle for the Mind 65

Ch. 7 Walking in Freedom.. 81

Ch. 8 Building in the Spirit... 93

Ch. 9 Walking Through Trials 103

Ch. 10 Walking in Family Life 115

Ch. 11 Walking in the Work Place 131

Ch. 12 The New Man 141

Ch. 13 The 'Flesh' and the 'Spirit' 151

Ch. 14 Walking in the Spirit 159

FOREWORD

The Apostle Paul offers as the key to successful Christian living the instruction "walk in the Spirit".

That may sound simple, yet through the years I have found it requires much of us in faith, character, knowledge and determination. As both a believer and a pastor I have experienced and seen the struggle involved in such a walk. Yet it remains a great key to making our lives in Christ victorious and effective.

Alison Chant brings to her writing on this subject not only her knowledge but also her experience. She is a woman that walks in the Spirit and as such writes from the depth of one who has travelled the path.

Alison is a wife, a mother and minister of God in her own right. She brings to her subject time spent as a local church pastor's wife, a counsellor, Bible College dean and a leader in God's Kingdom.

Her book is biblical, practical and proven. It is real, not simply motivational. Above all it is truth for everyday life.

As you read you will be guided in this walk in the Spirit by one who has gone before and who lives in joyous fellowship of the Spirit of God.

As her pastor and friend I commend Alison for her book and for her everyday example of Walking in the Spirit.

Grant Redman

Pastor

New Horizon Community Church

Sydney, Australia

PREFACE

Walking in the Spirit, in the awareness, the blessing, and the counsel of God is the desire of every earnest Christian.

It was no mistake that the desert loomed large in the lives of the prophets of God, who lived for his presence. Jesus also withdrew into the desert, endured the temptations of Satan and came out again empowered by God.

The desert has a way of concentrating the faculties, of making one aware of the overwhelming enormity of God in his omnipotence. The stars loom large and luminous in the night sky. Blazing with the glory of God, far away from city lights and polluted air that would dim their shining, they press down on the soul. They are an illustration of God's greatness and our smallness; our dependency; our isolation from the cosmos.

Little wonder men and women streamed into desert regions to get closer to God, many spending years in contemplation, only to realise finally their obligation to return to the world of men and fulfil the command of Christ to feed, clothe, heal, and teach.

In this busy modern world it has become increasingly hard for Christians to find the time and the isolation to meditate on the things of God. Too many allow themselves to be caught up with the seemingly important, necessary, even urgent tasks of their lives leaving aside the essential, fundamental task of getting to know God intimately.

But if we can discipline ourselves to spend the necessary time we can be constantly aware of God even in the midst of our busy-ness.

In the gospels we see Jesus daily drawing aside for communion with his Father so he could say,

> *I did not speak of my own accord, but the Father who sent me commanded me what to say and how to say it. I know that his command leads to eternal life. So whatever I say is just what the Father has told me to say* (Jn 12:49-50).

We too need to live in this dimension so that we can truly say, '**We are Christians who walk in the Spirit.**'

In this book, 'Walking in the Spirit' is examined from many different aspects concluding with teaching on 'The New Man.'

CHAPTER ONE

HOW WE SHOULD LIVE

A satire is a literary work holding up human vices and follies to ridicule and scorn. Malcolm Muggeridge (a news reporter of the 20th century) satirised the affluence of the West, its materialism, superficiality, and selfishness.

I) THE 'ME' GENERATION

Wealth increasing forevermore, and its beneficiaries, rich in hire purchase, stupefied with the 'telly' and with sex, comprehensively educated, told by Professor Hoyle how the world began and by Bertrand Russell where it will end; venturing forth on the broad highways, three lanes a side ... blood spattering the tarmac as an extra thrill; heaven lying about them in the super market, the rainbow ending in the nearest bingo hall, leisure burgeoning out in multitudinous shining aerials rising like dreaming spires into the sky; ... many mansions, mansions of light and chromium, climbing ever upwards. This kingdom surely can only be for posterity an unending source of wry derision – always assuming there is to be any posterity. The backdrop, after all, is the mushroom cloud; as the

Gadarene herd frisk and frolic, they draw ever nearer to the cliff's precipitous edge.[1]

How should we live in this world of the 'me' generation where so much selfishness abounds? The Apostle Peter answers the question:

> *But the day of the Lord will come like a thief. The heavens will disappear with a roar; the elements will be destroyed by fire, and the earth and everything in it will be laid bare. Since everything will be destroyed in this way, what kind of people ought you to be? You ought to live holy and godly lives as you look forward to the day of God and speed its coming* (2 Pe 3:10-12a).

Are we as shocked by sin as we used to be? Have we become more and more tolerant toward evil? The world is full of violence, the tide of sin is rising, and we are surrounded by vice in all its ugliness. Unnatural affection, parents divorcing, others abandoning their children, pornography becoming more easily obtained through the internet, gang rapes, murder, dishonesty, occult practices. The Apostle Paul saw it all clearly.

> *But mark this: There will be terrible times in the last days. People will be lovers of themselves, lovers of money, boastful, proud, abusive, disobedient to their parents, ungrateful, unholy, without love, unforgiving, slanderous, without self control, brutal, not lovers of the good, treacherous, rash, conceited, lovers of pleasure rather than lovers of God – having a form of godliness but denying its power. Have nothing to do with them* (2 Ti 3:1-5).

---

1) John Stott; *Issues Facing Christians Today*, pg 212.

How can we walk in the Spirit within our present culture?

Surrounded as we are by the pressures to conform, how carefully we need to weigh each decision we make. Each one must be a godly decision, one that will steer us toward holiness and not away from it; toward God and not away from him or from the godly principles by which he wants us to live.

II) WHAT KIND OF PERSONS SHOULD WE BE?

A) WE SHOULD BE PURE IN HEART

> *Blessed are the pure in heart for they will see God (Mt 5:8).*

> *And this is my prayer: that your love may abound more and more in knowledge and depth of insight, so that you may be able to discern what is best and may be pure and blameless until the day of Christ, filled with the fruit of righteousness that comes through Jesus Christ – to the glory and praise of God* (Ph 1:9-11).

The Greek word for 'pure', *katharos* means 'unmixed'; 'unadulterated'. This word is used in reference to corn (sifted), metal (pure), clothing (one type, such as cotton), and also to the Greek army. A Greek army that was *katharos* was one purged of all discontented, cowardly, unwilling or inefficient, soldiers. A *katharos* army is an army of first-class fighting men, all of them contented, courageous, willing and efficient. We as Christians are privileged to belong to the *katharos* army of Christ, not only content in Christ but also strong.

> *Be on your guard; stand firm in the faith; be men of courage; be strong* (1Co 16:13).

> *I know what it is to be in need, and I know what it is to have plenty. I have learned the secret of being content in any and every situation, whether*

> *well fed or hungry, whether living in plenty or in want. I can do everything through him who gives me strength* (Ph 4:12-13).

We can be pure because sin no longer has dominion over us. We are set free from sin as we trust in the blood of Jesus, set free by his death and resurrection. He has promised that he will forgive our sin and cleanse us from all unrighteousness (1Jn1:8-9).

We are translated into his Kingdom and new laws prevail here, sin is blotted out and righteousness takes its place, you lose your life to save it, hate is changed to love; un-forgiveness to forgiveness. Purity can be yours, as you look to Jesus who has promised to present you to the Father blameless in that wonderful day when you stand in his presence.

Paul prays for this in 1 Th 5:23-24 and makes a faith statement that it will indeed happen!

> *May God himself, the God of peace, sanctify you through and through. May your whole spirit, soul and body be kept blameless at the coming of our Lord Jesus Christ. The one who calls you is faithful and he will do it.*

We cannot overcome sin by striving, but by resting in Christ, turning away from sin, putting off the old man and putting on the new man (Cl 3:5-17).

B) WE SHOULD BE PATIENT IN FAITH

> *We do not want you to become lazy, but to imitate those who through **faith** and **patience** inherit what has been promised* (He 6:12).

> *So do not throw away your confidence; it will be richly rewarded. You need to **persevere** so that when you have done the will of God, you will receive what he has promised* (He 10:35-36).

Perseverance or endurance is that **extra inner strength**, with the ability to continue on even when everything seems to be against us. We must be **patient in faith**, not giving up too soon, enduring until we see the answer to our believing prayer.

> *...the seed on good soil stands for those with a noble and good heart, who hear the word, retain it, and by **persevering** produce a crop* (Lu 8:15).

As we walk in the Spirit we can witness for the Lord and bear fruit in souls saved and brought into the Kingdom of God, and in our daily life we can bear the fruit of the Spirit for the glory of God.

C) WE SHOULD BE PERSISTENT IN SERVICE

> *'Come to me, all you who are weary and burdened, and I will give you rest. Take my yoke upon you and learn from me, for I am gentle and humble in heart, and you will find rest for your souls. For my yoke is **easy** and my burden is light'* (Mt 11:28).

The Greek word for 'easy' *(chrestos)* means **easy, well-fitting**. So in essence Jesus is saying,

> Wear my yoke for it fits perfectly, the life I give you to live is not a burden, but is made to measure to fit you. [2]

If we acknowledge Jesus as Lord he will send us work to do which fits our needs and abilities exactly. A task, **made to measure for us**.

When we give our life to God in service this is also part of our worship. Our service becomes worship when we engage in it **as**

---

2) William Barclay; *The Daily Study Bible*; Gospel of Matthew Vol. 2; St. Andrew Press, Edinburgh, 1963. Pg.19.

unto him.

> *Whatever you do, work at it with all your heart, as working for the Lord, not for men, since you know that you will receive an inheritance from the Lord as a reward. It is the Lord Christ you are serving* (Cl 3:23-24).

D) WE SHOULD BE POWERFUL IN PRAYER

> *The prayer of a righteous man is powerful and effective* (Ja 5:16b).

James is referring here to Elijah who was an ordinary person, possibly a farmer or shepherd, but he was a man filled with the Holy Spirit and he knew how to pray. He looked around him at the apostasy of his countrymen who had forgotten their God and were worshipping other gods. He knew from the Hebrew Scriptures that if the Israelites fell away from their worship of God that they would suffer drought. They had been warned!

> *Be careful, or you will be enticed to turn away and worship other gods and bow down to them. Then the Lord's anger will burn against you, and he will shut the heavens so that it will not rain and the ground will yield no produce, and you will soon perish from the good land the Lord is giving you* (De 11:16-17).

He saw the sin rampant around him and remembered the word of the Lord. He began to pray that God would send drought, otherwise he knew the people would look upon God as weak! When he had prayed and knew that he had a word from the Lord he was as bold as a lion.

> *Now Elijah the Tishbite, from Tishbe in Gilead, said to Ahab, 'As the Lord, the God of Israel, lives, whom I serve, there will be neither dew nor*

rain in the next few years except at my word' (1 Kings 17:1).

He went, just as he was, bold and unafraid, into the court of King Ahab.

If you have prayed through in the will of God you will also be able to do the task God has given you boldly and courageously.

1). Elijah gave three indications of the source of his strength.

*a) **As the Lord, the God of Israel, lives** –* To Elijah God was the supreme reality, more real than what he could see with his physical eye.

Jesus, and the heavenly spiritual realm, should be as real to us as this physical realm. Indeed more real, as it is eternal and this physical realm that appears to us to be so solid will one day be burned up (2 Pe 3:10).

*b) **Whom I serve,** –* Elijah was standing in an earthly court but to him God's heavenly court was even more real; he was serving, not an earthly king, but the Lord of hosts (Re 4:1-8).

To have this same vision will lift us above fear, and the fear of man will not hold us back from doing the will of God. We are God's chosen messengers and have been given our commission (Mt 28:18-20).

c) **Elijah's name means 'God is my strength'.** God is also our strength, with him we are more than conquerors (Ro 8:37-39). We should be like Elijah in the way we live our lives before the world so we will be able to say with the ransomed saints.

(We) overcame (Satan) by the blood of the lamb and by the word of (our) testimony (Re 12:11a).

Christians are often defeated in the spiritual battles of life because they do not know the rules for victory. <u>God has revealed these rules in clear terms</u>. Battles are not won by lectures on weapons but as we clash with the enemy and fight and overcome him

2) In Ephesians 6:10-18 God lays out the battle plan through Paul his mighty apostle. We are to be strong in the Lord and in his mighty power and we are to put on the full armour of God. Then we are to take our stand against the devil and all of his deceitful scheming. It is a spiritual power we are called to withstand and we cannot do this alone, God has made provision for us.

3) We are to stand for the truth, relying on the righteousness Christ has wrought for us on the cross. We must be ready to call people to the gospel, to be a living witness of the good news that God loves them and has a plan for their life. We are to strengthen our faith by using it constantly to protect us from the fiery darts of temptation which come from the enemy of our souls. We are to place on our head the helmet of salvation and take up the sword of the Spirit, the Word of the living God, and we must learn to wield this weapon by speaking it aloud and claiming our authority over the enemy of our souls. Finally, we are to remember to pray in the Spirit constantly lest we allow the enemy to get a foothold in our life.

4) God educates us to pray powerfully and there are three lessons we can learn from Elijah.

a) **Take one step at a time**. God gives strength and faith for each day. If we endeavour to look too far ahead we may falter. He gave Elijah one task at a time gradually increasing the power he trusted him with until Mt Carmel's amazing scene was played out and the priests of Baal were overcome (1Kg 18:16-45).

b) **Learn the value of times of rest.** Sometimes God lays us aside for a season. Perhaps to teach humility, perhaps so that we do not overdo and leave ourselves open to sickness. This laying aside for a season makes us realise that we can do nothing of ourselves and ensures that when we do complete something for God we are careful to give him all the glory (1Kg 17:2-7).

c) **Learn to trust God absolutely, no matter what happens**. Through many years of Christian life we should learn to trust God without wavering. Even if at times it may appear that he has not met our need, we will find on looking back over our past that indeed he has been faithful, though perhaps in a different way from our expectations. If we make sure we are in God's will, we can know he will meet us at the point of our need as he met Elijah in his despair and gave to him a new commission(1 Kg 19:1-18).

> "God's work, done in God's way, will never lack God's blessing" [3]

5) For what quality of life should we aim?

A life of holiness: separated from the world, separated unto God. A life of godliness; God-like-ness, we should live, as far as we are able, in the way Jesus would live if he were in our place, working at our job, faced with our decisions. Walking in the Spirit we should maintain a purity of heart, be persistent in our service for God and learn to pray powerfully.

We will examine prayer more fully in the next chapter.

---

3) Quote from Hudson Taylor, the founder of The China Inland Mission.

CHAPTER TWO

HOW WE SHOULD PRAY

Part of the life of walking in the Spirit is being ready at all times to pray for others who are in need, but God will not release us to pray effectively for others until we have confessed all our own sin. We must be confident that we are forgiven and cleansed before we pray.

> *If I had cherished sin in my heart, the Lord would not have listened* (Ps 66:18).

> *Surely the arm of the Lord is not too short to save, nor his ear too dull to hear. But your iniquities have separated you from your God; your sins have hidden his face from you, so that he will not hear* (Is 59:1-2).

> *For the eyes of the Lord are on the righteous and his ears are attentive to their prayer, but the face of the Lord is against those who do evil* (1 Pe 3:12).

> *If we confess our sins, he is faithful and just and will forgive us our sins and purify us from all unrighteousness* (1 Jn 1:9).

A) FORGIVEN

We must have a clear conscience if we are going to be faith

warriors and petition God to answer our prayers. If our conscience is troubling us then we will not be able to feel complete confidence in God (1Jn 3:21-22).

When we pray for others we must be sure Satan cannot find anything with which to accuse us. Jesus had this confidence as he told his disciples in Jn 14:30:

> *'I will not speak with you much longer, for the prince of this world is coming.* **He has no hold on me***'.*

Once we have confessed all known sin then we must believe we have forgiveness otherwise we will paralyse our prayer life by constant worry, doubt and continual self-effort.

B) FORGIVING

Unforgiveness on our part can also block our prayers from being answered. Jesus made this very clear in Mark 11:25 –

> *And when you stand praying, if you hold anything against anyone, forgive him, so that your Father in heaven may forgive you your sins.*

If we do not forgive we will not be forgiven, as Jesus so eloquently warned in his parable of the unjust servant (Mt 18:21-35), and in Luke he gives us the rule of forgiveness which the disciples found hard to understand, indeed they begged Jesus to increase their faith so they could live by it.

> *If your brother sins, rebuke him, and if he repents, forgive him. If he sins against you seven times in a day, and seven times comes back to you and says, 'I repent,' forgive him (Lu 17:3-4).*

Even more, if we do not forgive, we effectively block our own prayers from being answered. Elton Trueblood, writes:

The limitation on the power of prayer is not natural law. It is the lack of forgiveness on the part of the one who prays.[4]

C) FAITH

Now faith is being sure of what we hope for and certain of what we do not see (He 11:1).

Faith is the assurance of what we hope for, the proof of what we do not see. Faith is the substance (Gr. *hupostasis* – 'assurance', 'confidence'). Faith is the evidence (Gr. *elenchos* – 'proof', 'proving', 'test').

In the Interpreter's Bible this explanation is given for the text:

> In the Bible faith means trust as well as belief. The man of faith commits to Jesus Christ his mind and heart, his obedience and destiny, himself. When Jesus said, '*My food is to do the will of him who sent me, and to accomplish his work,*' that was faith.

What can we learn about faith, the kind of faith that will ensure answers to our prayers?

1) Our faith must rest solely in God and must not be influenced by outward circumstances, that is things we can see and hear with our natural senses. We must see instead God, his angels, his power, his victory, and his omnipotence.

2) Jesus, our example, was not troubled by natural laws because he had perfect trust in God who created those laws. Jesus, the Son of God, transcended natural law, he walked on water (Mk

---

4) Elton Trueblood Ph.D. was a Quaker Scholar; A graduate of Harvard USA (1900-1994) he wrote *The Yoke of Christ* 1958; *The Company of the Committed* 1961; *The People Called Quakers* 1966 and *The Validity of Christian Mission* 1972.

6:47-52), multiplied the loaves and the fish (Mk 6:35-44) and healed all manner of disease (Mt 8:16-17).

3) God is Lord of natural law. Therefore he can move over and above it, change it, use it, accelerate its working as he pleases. Miracles are instant healings, and God is able to restore body parts, such as kidneys, through a miracle of his power and ability.

4) Our faith must be like that of a child. We must exhibit the same perfect trust that the mighty men of OT times radiated, like the courage shown by Daniel and his friends Shadrach, Meshach and Abednego (Da 3:16-18; 6:16-23).

Daniel believed and God preserved his life in the den of lions because, he said,

> *'My God sent his angel, and he shut the mouths of the lions. They have not hurt me, because I was found innocent in his sight. Nor have I done any wrong before you, O king'.*

Shadrach Meshach and Abednego also knew they were innocent and they put their lives into God's hands. They were not afraid of king Nebuchadnezzar, nor of the fiery furnace that he had prepared for them, and they were vindicated by a mighty miracle of divine power. The king was overcome with amazement and said,

> *'Look! I see four men walking around in the fire, unbound and unharmed, and the fourth looks like a son of the gods.'*

In this same way, if we are innocent, having confessed all known sin to the Lord and been forgiven because of the blood of Jesus that he shed for us; if our conscience is clear; then our faith in God will be strong.

5) Hearing God through his Word begets an absolute trust in God, in who he is, and in his great power and ability.

6) Meditation on his Word will lead to a bold and courageous spirit such as Elijah had (1 Kgs. chs. 17-19).

7) Faith also comes from contemplating what God has done in history with Abraham, Joseph, David, Elijah, Elisha, and others, up to the present day. Reading about the lives and the exploits of great men and women of God such as Luther, John Calvin, John Wesley, Alexander Dowie, John G. Lake, Smith Wigglesworth, Maria Woodworth Etter, Evangeline Booth and many others, increases our faith.

8) Finally faith grows through action, we must put our faith into action. If we don't exercise our faith it will not develop. We all have faith, it is up to us how strong that faith becomes.

> *I say to every one of you: do not think of yourself more highly than you ought, but rather think of yourself with sober judgment, in accordance with the measure of faith God has given you* (Ro 12:3).

D) CONFIDENCE

> *So do not throw away your confidence, it will be richly rewarded* (He 10:35).

This is what we need to do; trust in God whose character is holy and whose ability and power is awesome. We can never plumb the depths of God's strength, or the height of his love for us.

We must have confidence in him (Gr. *pepoithesis* – 'persuasion', 'assurance', 'trust').

In Webster's Dictionary 'confidence' means 'faith' or 'trust' (in God's mercy) or in oneself and 'trust' means 'having assured reliance on the character, ability, strength or truth of someone or something'.

> *You need to persevere so that when you have done the will of God you will receive what he has promised* (vs 36).

We must persevere (Gr. *hupomeno* – 'to abide under', 'to bear up courageously under suffering', also translated 'patient', 'endure').

In Webster's 'abide' means to endure without yielding; to bear patiently; to remain stable or fixed in state.

What does this mean for us?

1) We must have the patience to continue praying for as long a time as necessary. Some prayers are answered immediately, some take days, weeks, months, even years.

2) After first discovering God's will in the matter then we can pray effectually (Ja 5:16b). It is no use for us to pray for something if we know from God's Word that it is not his will.

Effectually meaning 'the effect produced in the praying man, bringing him into line with the will of God', as in the case of Elijah. [5]

So, if necessary, God changes us as we pray; we are conformed or moulded to his will, as we pray.

3) God's faithfulness never ceases, if we continue steadfast he will answer and he will not fail us.

> *Because of the Lord's great love we are not consumed, for his compassions never fail, they are new every morning; great is your faithfulness* (La 3:22-26).

---

5) W. E. Vine; *An Expository Dictionary of NT Words;* Oliphants, Blundell House. London. 'effectual' Vol. ll; E-Li, pg.19.

E) THE MOST IMPORTANT TASK

The most important thing for any Christian is to find the will of God for their life and then do it

> *Do not conform any longer to the pattern of this world, but be transformed by the renewing of your mind. Then you will be able to test and approve what God's will is – his good, pleasant, and perfect will* (Ro 12:1-2).

> *The world and its desires pass away, but the man who does the will of God lives forever* (1 Jn 2:17).

Study God's Word and follow the directions; God will reveal things to you as you read. He does not expect you to know it all at once but to obey each part as he makes it clear to you.

Waiting time is preparation time, so learn to wait for God's timing; he will close doors until you are prepared and he will open doors when you are ready.

God will give you confirmation, through his Word, through prophecy, through circumstances, through counsel from pastor and friends, through peace in your heart.

Success in prayer comes when:

- we find God's will
- we wait God's timing
- we trust God
- we are willing to obey God
- we wait for confirmation
- we allow God to prepare us for the task, and we do what we can to prepare ourselves

F) GOD CAN USE ANYONE

You may feel you have no special talent, but even so you may be the means of bringing someone to Christ who then becomes a great evangelist or a great teacher! Andrew brought Simon who later became Peter, one of the foremost apostles (Jn 1:40-42).

God looks on the heart and he is looking for willing and obedient people to serve him. Those who will seek to obey and please him in all they do; those who will continue to trust him until the work is done, the prayers are granted, or the task is made clear.

God can use Christians anywhere if they are willing to walk in the Spirit, we must live for God in whatever sphere he places us.

CHAPTER THREE

GAINING CHARACTER

Elizabeth Kotlowski in her book, *South-Land of the Holy Spirit* has given us many pen- sketches of famous early Australian explorers-

John McDouall Stuart (1815-1866) was the first explorer to reach the centre of Australia. It was on his fourth exploration he achieved his heart's desire. On the 23rd of April 1860 he placed the British flag on Central Mt Stuart. He was also the first to discover an all-season route, from Adelaide in the south to Darwin in the north; which was later used for the Overland Telegraph.

> Stuart was a man of indomitable perseverance and courage. Though his sufferings were sometimes intolerable he would not give up. One of the exploration party, William Patrick Auld, said, 'I don't believe any other man could or would have travelled with the frightful agonies that Stuart suffered.'... He suffered from scurvy and the intense heat. His eyes were so painful, that there were some days he could not see. He was near death several times, and he never fully recovered his health.

Stuart acknowledged his reliance on God as excerpts from his journal show - :

> The sky is overcast and I trust that Providence will send us rain in the morning.
>
> About an hour before sundown, they arrived at the water, without any more losses, for which I sincerely thank God.
>
> (And on his safe return from the expedition):
>
> I sincerely thank the Almighty Disposer of Events that he, in his infinite goodness and mercy, gave me strength and courage ... and has kindly permitted me to live yet a little longer. [6]

John McDouall Stuart was an example of strong and resolute Christian character. His perseverance, courage and faith in the face of tremendous hardships places him among the great men of Australia.

To walk in the Spirit requires character and the way to gain that is through the power of choice.

A) THE POWER OF CHOICE.

The Greek word for 'character' is almost the same as our English word – *'charakter'*. It means **the seat of one's moral being.**

- It is shown by the actions of an individual when under pressure.
- It is the combination of the qualities which distinguish a person.
- In the KJV it is translated as 'image'.

---

6) Elizabeth Rogers Kotlowski; *South-Land of the Holy Spirit-A Christian History of Australia*; Published by Christian History Research Inst. Orange NSW. Pgs. 198-200.

- It is a distinctive mark impressed by an outward force, as of a sharp instrument gouging marks [7]

How can we form our Christian character?

1) Know yourself, who you are, what makes you do the things you do, why you have the opinions you have. Current thinking agrees that we are all a mixture throughout our life of our genes and our environment. There are many books that help to explore these issues.[8]

2) Know who you are in God.

First, we are God's children, he has given us permission to become part of his family (Jn 1:12), we are his priests and part of his holy temple (1Pe 2:4-5).

Second, we must search out and follow God's principles. <u>A principle is a truth, method or rule adopted as the basis for action or conduct</u>. A biblical principle is a spiritual truth taught in Scripture. Looking into the Word of God, we search out the principles of God, and then incorporate them into our life. The greatest principle is found in Mt 22:37.

> *Love the Lord your God with all your heart, with all your soul, and with all your mind ... the second is like it, 'Love your neighbour as yourself'.*

Two more are – *Give, and it will be given to you* (Lu 6:38).

---

7) Stan DeKoven; *Leadership-Vision for the City*, Vision Publishing; 1994.

8) One such book is: Florence Littauer; *Personality Plus;* Fleming H. Revell; 2001.

> *Seek first his kingdom and his righteousness, and all these things will be given to you as well* (Mt 6:33).

God has also promised to write his laws on our hearts (Je 31:33).

> *'This is the covenant I will make with the house of Israel after that time,' declares the Lord. 'I will put my law in their minds and write it on their hearts. I will be their God, and they will be my people.'*

3) Learn discipline.

Hugo Grotius (1654) had this to say about the discipline needed to form character –

> He knows not how to rule a kingdom, that cannot manage a province; nor can he wield a province, that cannot order a city; nor he order a city, that knows not how to regulate a village; nor he a village, that cannot guide a family; nor can that man govern well a family that knows not how to govern himself; neither can any govern himself unless his reason be Lord, will and appetite his vassals; nor can reason rule unless herself be governed by God, and wholly obedient to him. [9]

Grotius shows us two types of government, one external and the other internal. For a man to govern an external body of men, or even his own family, he must first know how to govern his own passions and he himself must be governed internally by God's laws.

Therefore we must be able to govern ourselves

---

9) Quote from Hugo Grotius, also called Huig de Groot; poet and theologian 1583-1645.

> *Better a patient man than a warrior, a man who controls his temper than one who takes a city* (Pr 16:32).

If we are willing God will assist us in the forming of our character because he will use those things that happen to us in our daily lives to mould us into the image of Christ (Ro 8:28).

What can stop us from forming a sound Christian character?

B) ANGER

James points out one thing that can stop us from forming a strong Christlike character:

> *Everyone should be quick to listen, slow to speak and slow to become angry, for man's anger does not bring about the righteous life that God desires. Therefore get rid of all moral filth and the evil that is so prevalent and humbly accept the word planted in you, which can save you. Do not merely listen to the word, and so deceive yourselves. Do what it says.* (Ja 1:20,22).

Anger can be righteous, and we know that Jesus was sometimes angry. He was angry with the money changers in the temple (Mt 21:12), and he was angry with the scribes and Pharisees when they opposed him (Mt 23:13-36).

In fact sometimes it can be a sin not to get angry, such as when we are confronted with child prostitution or slavery. This kind of anger is given to us to move us to do something about the problem; it is not a sin.

Sinful anger, that we are advised against, is the kind that continues over more than a day, the kind of anger that turns into resentment and bitterness and goes on and on. This kind of anger can be dangerous.

> Anger is so extraordinarily energetic, it involves the body from top to bottom. Under the influence of anger all the chemistry changes; tensions rise, pulse rate rises, blood pressure goes up, pupils dilate – and if this energy is not released, if it is held back in the body, then it starts off by causing structural damage: let not the sun go down upon one's wrath is an aphorism one really must take to heart. [10]

From another view point, note the difference between a candle and a bushfire. The same breeze which can blow out a candle can make a deadly, roaring furnace out of a bushfire.

One of the things we can do about anger is to work out ahead of time the kind of things that make us angry, such as lying, betrayal, or controlling people – we all have something that makes us fume. Looking ahead to defuse the times when anger may be a problem, by working out what to do to avoid those situations, will help in putting off anger and putting on a more appropriate fruit of the Spirit (Ga 5:23).

Sometimes anger can be masked and Dr. DeKoven in his book, *Marriage and Family Life,* covers this problem – [11]

> Because Christians feel guilty about anger, they may rephrase their responses, saying they are 'hurt'. Others will rephrase it as being 'disappointed', 'frustrated', or 'disturbed'. Some even deny the presence of anger, even though it may be apparent to others. There is a great need for being honest here. This is the first step in resolving anger which can build bridges to

---

10) Patricia Wendorf; *I Believe in Angels.*

11) Stan DeKoven; *Marriage and Family Life*; Vision Publishing 1998. pg.105.

communication rather than walls against each other ... It is not having the feeling of anger that is sin, but it is what we do with it. When anger becomes wrath, when we attack or say foolish things to hurt, this is sinful.

Anger can even sometimes be recycled, we can deceive ourselves, it can manifest as criticism, or sarcasm. You need to be honest, work out what makes you angry. Why is this? What can I do about it? Is it righteous or unrighteous anger? Understanding ourselves will go a long way toward clearing our anger and making us able to rather show the character of Jesus.

Should we pray to be rid of anger? This is not what Paul advises us to do. Instead he tells us to 'put off anger'. It is a choice we make, a choice to be more patient, kind and loving.

A word of warning

We can have problems if we spend too much time crying out to God for deliverance from anger and the other things that bind and hinder us from walking in the Spirit. It is a psychological fact that the more we concentrate on and think about our weaknesses, even in prayer to the Father, the more power they will gain in our life. No! We must turn away from them and toward putting on the character of Christ.

Put away the sins of the flesh and allow the Holy Spirit to produce the fruit of the Spirit in your life to replace anger or other negative weaknesses. Put away the negative and think on the positive truths of God –

> *Put to death therefore whatever belongs to your earthly nature ... You used to walk in these ways, in the life you once lived. But now you must rid yourselves of all such things as these; anger, rage, malice, slander, and filthy language from your lips* (Cl 3:5-8).

> *Finally brothers, whatever is true, whatever is noble, whatever is right, whatever is pure, whatever is lovely, whatever is admirable, – if anything is excellent or praiseworthy- think about such things* (Ph 4:8).

We are to make the choice then to feel compassion, kindness, humility, gentleness and patience. We are to forgive one another; putting away those things that make us stumble, and instead live a life well pleasing to the Lord (Cl 3:12-14).

Here is another story from Kotlowski's book of an Australian pioneer woman who despite sorrow and deprivation rose up with character and dignity to make something beautiful of her life.

Georgiana Molloy (1805-1843) came to Australia with her husband John, a retired veteran of the battle of Waterloo. She had been devout and active in the Presbyterian Church back home, teaching Sunday School and helping wherever she could. She married Captain Malloy at the age of 24 and emigrated with him to Western Australia.

She gave birth to her first baby one week after arrival in a leaking tent while rain poured down. The baby died, but she turned to God for comfort. Later she lost another of her seven children in a drowning accident. She was lonely, her husband was often away on business but she carried on with a cheerful spirit. Here is a quote from her letter to a friend.

> The Lord is good and has shown himself to us in many wonderful instances.

In 1836 she received a request for some samples of the local flora and this collecting became her hobby. For the next seven years she collected seeds and pressed flowers. The Aborigines also told her of medicinal herbs. In time she became known as the 'Madonna of the Bush' and the leading botanist throughout Western Australia.

> What had seemed like a wilderness to others became the 'Garden of Eden' to Mrs Malloy. To the end she sang a hymn of praise to God for all the beauty she had discovered in the Western Australian Bush. The tall scented Boronia Molloya was named after her." [12]

This true story, and the one at the beginning of this chapter, show people who were able to rise above their circumstances and, by making the choice to look to the Lord for their comfort and deliverance, they have left us with a legacy to look up to and to emulate. Neither one blamed God for their troubles, instead they proceeded with their lives, trusting in God to use their circumstances to show courage and fortitude, and to display the sweetness of the character of Christ. Both of them learned the stability that comes to the Christian who walks in the Spirit'.

How differently we see some Christians behaving today. The least sign of hardship and they are ready to abandon God and the church.

Looking into the Word of God we see ourselves as we are, we see what we can be, and we go on to believe the Word and make it work in our lives. We make choices to put the old life behind and to live the new life in Christ, choosing to build strong Christian character that can stand against any opposition.

---

12) Kotlowski op. cit. pgs. 226-227.

CHAPTER FOUR

PLEASING GOD

Paul Tournier was the son of a well known Geneva preacher, His father died when he was three months old and his mother when he was six years of age. He was brought up by an aunt and his consequent loneliness gave him empathy for others. He decided to become a doctor and practised in Geneva until his retirement. He became a Christian through the Oxford Group [13] and became convinced that treating people physically without treating their spiritual ailments was inadequate. So he developed his idea of 'medicine of the person' and wrote to all his patients telling them that from then on he would be treating them with a mixture of psychology, faith and medicine. He began to write about his experiences of holistic medicine in practice. His books have now sold millions of copies in 16 languages.

This is a quote from his book *'The Adventure of Living.'*

> For the fulfilment of his purpose God needs more than priests, bishops, pastors, and missionaries. He needs mechanics and chemists, gardeners and street sweepers, dressmakers and cooks, tradesmen, physicians, philosophers, judges, and short hand typists ... I do not serve God only in

---

[13] A group of influential Christians established at Oxford University in England; 1833.

the brief moments during which I am taking part in a religious service, or reading the Bible, or saying my prayers, or talking about him in some book I am writing, or discussing the meaning of life with a patient or a friend. I serve him quite as much when I am giving a patient an injection, or lancing an abscess, or writing a prescription, or giving a piece of good advice. Or again I serve him quite as much when I am reading the newspaper, travelling, laughing at a joke, or soldering a joint in an electric wire. I serve him by taking an interest in everything, because he is interested in everything, because he has created everything and has put me in his creation so that I might participate in it fully. 'It is a great mistake', wrote Archbishop William Temple, 'to suppose that God is interested only, or even primarily, in religion. [14]

So what has this to do with 'walking in the Spirit?'

Walking in the Spirit does not mean being mystical, or too heavenly minded to be any earthly use! Instead we are told that whatever we do in word or deed should be done in the name of Jesus (Cl 3:17). So if the word or deed we are contemplating is something we can't do in the name of Jesus, if it's something that disturbs our conscience, then it is definitely not 'walking in the Spirit.'

Our motto should rather be; **Help me Lord to be intensely spiritual but also definitely practical.**

So how should we define 'Walking in the Spirit?'

---

14) Veronica Zundel (compiled); *Eerdman's Book of Christian Classics;* William B. Eerdman's Pub. Co.1988. pg. 103.

A) WALKING IN HIS STEPS

We are to walk in the steps of Jesus, he is our example! We should seek to please him, as he himself pleased his Father. Jesus said of himself,

> *The one who sent me is with me; he has not left me alone, for I always do what pleases him (Jn 8:29).*

There are Scriptures throughout the Bible that inspire us to please the Lord and in Ephesians Paul encourages us to find out what pleases him.

> *For you were once darkness, but now you are light in the Lord. Live as children of light (for the fruit of the light consists of all goodness, righteousness and truth).***and find out what pleases the Lord (Ep 5:8-10).**

John the beloved disciple gives us instructions for obtaining answers to prayer, which include this idea of pleasing the Lord and also obeying his commands –

> *This then is how we know that we belong to the truth, and how we set our hearts at rest in his presence whenever our hearts condemn us. For God is greater than our hearts, and he knows everything. Dear friends, if our hearts do not condemn us, we have confidence before God and receive from him anything we ask,* **because we obey his commands and do what pleases him** (1 Jn 3:19-22).

B) PLEASING GOD

There are many verses that indicate the things that please the Lord, here are a few:

1) We should ask God to teach us his ways as Moses did in Exodus 33.

> *Moses said to the Lord, You have been telling me 'lead these people,' but you have not let me know whom you will send with me. You have said, 'I know you by name and you have found favour with me.' If you are pleased with me, teach me your ways so I may know you and continue to find favour with you. Remember that this nation is your people. The Lord replied, 'My Presence will go with you, and I will give you rest.' Then Moses said to him, 'If your presence does not go with us, do not send us up from here. How will anyone know you are pleased with me and with your people unless you go with us? What else will distinguish me and your people from all the other people on the face of the earth?' And the Lord said to Moses, 'I will do the very thing you have asked, because I am pleased with you and I know you by name* (Ex 33:12-17).

2) Our worship, praise and thanksgiving are pleasing to the Lord,

> *I will praise God's name in song and glorify him with thanksgiving. This will please the Lord more than an ox, more than a bull with its horns and hoofs* (Ps 69:30-31).

3) Our prayers and intercessions give him pleasure,

> *The Lord detests the sacrifice of the wicked, but the prayer of the upright pleases him* (Pr 15:8).

4) The Lord is pleased with our faith, in fact we cannot please him without it

> *And without faith it is impossible to please God, because anyone who comes to him must believe that he exists and that he rewards those who earnestly seek him* (He 11:6).

5) Paul instructs us in 1 Thessalonians 4:1-12 how to live in order to please God. He explains that it is God's will for us to be sanctified; that we should learn to control our body. We should not wrong our brothers and sisters in Christ, but instead we should love one another. We should make it our ambition to lead a quiet life, minding our own business, working with our hands and supporting ourselves. He goes on to warn that anyone who rejects these instructions does not reject man but God.

C) REWARDS FOR PLEASING GOD

> *If the Lord is pleased with us, he will lead us into that land, a land flowing with milk and honey, and will give it to us* (Nu 14:8).

We see here in 'type' that if the Lord is pleased with us he will lead us into the depths of revelation of his Word and into the sweetness of his presence. In effect he will give himself to us in sweet fellowship and will commune with us and teach us his ways.

David was confident in God:

> *I know that you are pleased with me, for my enemy does not triumph over me. In my integrity you uphold me and set me in your presence for ever* (Ps 41:11-12).

The warrior king, despite his blunders, was also the sweet singer of Israel, he was a man after God's own heart for he had great faith and knew how to encourage himself in the Lord. Because of his example we can believe that our enemy, Satan, will not triumph over us and that we too will dwell in the presence of the Lord forever.

The wise man, **Solomon**, promises us wisdom, knowledge and happiness if we please God, three goals eminently to be desired.

> *To the man who pleases him, God gives wisdom, knowledge and happiness ...* (Ec 2:26a).

D) OBEDIENCE IS BETTER

As well as seeking to please the Lord we are told by John that we should **obey his commands** if we desire our prayers to be answered. There are around 49 general commands of Christ in the Gospels, but he also said that the greatest consisted in loving God and our neighbour.

> *The most important (command), answered Jesus, is this: Hear O Israel, the Lord our God, the Lord is one. Love the Lord your God with all your heart and with all your soul and with all your mind and with all your strength. The second is this: Love your neighbour as yourself. There is no commandment greater than these* (Mk 12:29-31).

Raniero Cantalamessa, a Catholic brother has this to say about obedience –

> The Greek term for obedience in the New Testament (*hypakouein*) literally translated means 'to listen carefully' or 'pay attention,' ... In its original significance, therefore, obedience means submission to the Word, recognising its real power over us. It is easy therefore to understand how a rediscovery of obedience must be kept in mind while we are in the process of rediscovering the Word of God in the church today. You cannot cultivate the Word of God without also cultivating obedience. Otherwise you become disobedient ipso facto.

Disobedience (*parakouein*) means listening carelessly, with distraction. We could say it means listening in a detached or neutral way without feeling in any way obliged to act on what is being listened to and thus reserving one's own power of decision. The disobedient are those who listen to the Word but, as Jesus said, do not act on it (Mt 7:26). They do not even feel obliged to act on it. They study the Word but without the idea of having to submit to it; they dominate the Word, in the sense that they master the critical tools and rules of analysis, but they do not want to be dominated; they want to maintain the neutrality proper to every scholar with regard to the object of his science. On the contrary, the way of obedience is open to those who have decided to live 'for the Lord'; it is a need that is released by true conversion. Just as the book of the 'Rules' to be observed is given to a newly professed religious so a newly converted Christian to the gospel, in the Holy Spirit, is given this simple rule: 'Be obedient! Obey the Word! 'Salvation lies in obedience. In the constant struggle between the two kingdoms only the ranks of the obedient will be saved and their password will be 'Obedience to God. [15]

1) The obedience of Christ

And being found in appearance as a man, he humbled himself and became obedient to death – even death on a cross! (Ph 2:8).

---

15) Raneiro Cantalamessa; *Life in the Lordship of Christ;* Darton, Longman & Todd. London. 1992; pgs. 232-233.

The true basis of Christian obedience is not an idea of obedience, but an act of obedience. It is not what we say, or even believe, that shows our obedience, but what we do to show that obedience in our daily life. This is based on the fact of Christ's obedience to his Father, he was obedient even though it meant, finally, his death on the cross.

Christ learned obedience through the things he suffered (He 5:8-9) and by his obedience we are made righteous (Ro 5:19). Obedience is as important as justification for without the obedience of Christ we would not be justified.

As Jesus grew he showed obedience, first to his parents, then to the Law, the Sanhedrin, and to Pilate, the Roman Governor. Then as his final act of obedience he went to the cross, paying the ultimate sacrifice for us who believe.

> Jesus said, *'My food is to do the will of him who sent me and to finish his work'* (Jn 4:34) and again, *'The one who sent me is with me; he has not left me alone,* **for *I always do what pleases him'*** (8:29).

Jesus carried out his obedience all through his life. He had no control over the events of his birth and flight into Egypt, but as he grew he resolved to obey the words in OT Scripture concerning himself over which he could show his perfect trust in his Father.

Jesus was careful to fulfil perfectly through his obedience all that was written of him in the Old Testament. When the disciples attempted to oppose his capture, Jesus said,

> *'Do you think I cannot call on my Father, and he will at once put at my disposal more than twelve legions of angels? But how then would the Scriptures be fulfilled that say it must happen in this way?'* (Mt 26:54).

2) Obedience brings the power of God

After his temptation in the wilderness Luke tells us that Jesus returned in the power of the Spirit (Lu 4:14). The Holy Spirit is given to those who obey God (Ac 5:32).

Throughout his life on earth Jesus proved his anointing, gained through his obedience, by the miracles he wrought.

> *God anointed Jesus of Nazareth with the Holy Spirit and power, and ... he went around doing good and healing all who were under the power of the devil, because God was with him* (Ac 10:38).

God honoured Christ by raising him from the dead, proving by this demonstration of power that Jesus was indeed his Son.

> *The gospel he promised beforehand through his prophets in the Holy Scriptures regarding his Son, who as to his human nature was a descendent of David, and who through the Spirit of holiness was declared to be the Son of God by his resurrection from the dead: Jesus Christ our Lord (Ro 1:2-4).*

3) Guidance for daily obedience.

There are times in our life when we would like to be obedient but are not sure what to do because there is no specific Scripture to guide and direct us. But if our purpose is to obey the Lord in every respect then we can trust him to guide us in the right way.

The foundation of all guidance, however, must be the Word of God already given.

If God has already revealed something to you in Scripture that answers your query then that is his will for you. Until you have searched out Scripture you must not ask or expect separate, direct, personal revelation.

> *... The sheep listen to his voice. He calls his own sheep by name and leads them out. When he has brought out all his own, he goes on ahead of them, and his sheep follow him, because they know his voice (Jn 10:3b-4).*
>
> *The Counselor, the Holy Spirit, whom the Father will send in my name, will teach you all things and will remind you of everything I have said to you (Jn 14:26).*
>
> *If any of you lacks wisdom, he should ask God, who gives generously to all without finding fault, and it will be given to him. But when he asks, he must believe and not doubt, ... (Ja 1:5-6a).*

With these Scriptures in mind we must believe that Divine Guidance is promised to us and our faith must therefore confidently look for and expect it, asking in faith without wavering.

However, if we aren't walking in the truth and in the right way, **we can block God from speaking to us**, so we must be careful to walk softly before the Lord. Whatever is of God he will quicken to us and we will not forget what he has told us.

There are four avenues through which God speaks to us –

- through the Scriptures,
- through providential circumstances,
- through the convictions of our own higher judgment and
- through the impressions of the Holy Spirit on our minds.

There are other voices apart from God who will attempt to guide us.

There are impressions from the strong personalities of those around us.

Sometimes impressions can arise from our physical condition.

Impressions can come from our demonic enemies because their voices are also from the spiritual realm.

Here are some words of wisdom about guidance from a Brethren lady, Hannah Whitall Smith (1832-1911), who died almost a hundred years ago, and whose book is still in print. In fact her book was so popular that, with her meetings and sermons on 'the higher Christian life', she was partly instrumental in the development of the Keswick Convention [16], an annual 'teach in' on holiness of life, which still continues today. Here is what she has to say on hearing the voices of our spiritual enemies:

> And finally, impressions come from those spiritual enemies which seem to lie in wait for every traveller who seeks to enter the higher regions of the spiritual life. In the same Epistle which tells us that we are 'seated in heavenly places' in Christ (Ep 2:6) we are also told that we shall have to fight there with spiritual enemies (Ep 6:12). These spiritual enemies, whoever or whatever they may be, must necessarily communicate with us by means of our spiritual faculties; and their voices therefore will be, as the voice of God is, an inward impression made upon our spirits. Consequently, just as the Holy Spirit may tell us by impressions what is the will of God concerning us, so also will these spiritual enemies tell us by impressions what is their will concerning us, disguising themselves, of course,

---

[16] This Christian Convention was begun through the ministry of USA evangelist Dwight L. Moody.

as 'angels of light' who have come to lead us closer to God. [17]

All leadings then must be tested by Scripture, by the principles and precepts of the Lord. If these all line up and harmonise together then we can be sure we are being led correctly.

But be clear concerning this one thing. **His word will always be in harmony with itself,** we cannot be told one thing which agrees with his Word and then another opposite to it. If the voices do not agree then they are not the same, one is from another source, either from our own imagination or from our enemy, the devil.

Sometimes we may have to wait patiently for God to make all things plain to us, it is dangerous to go ahead of God's plan. As we learn to trust him more fully we will see more clearly where he is leading, as he promised through the prophet Isaiah:

> *O people of Zion, who live in Jerusalem, you will weep no more. How gracious he will be when you cry for help! As soon as he hears, he will answer you* (Is 30:19).

Walking in the Spirit is not being mystical but practical. We should seek to please God in all we do and say and we should walk in obedience, being led continually by the Holy Spirit. We will examine more of the practical aspects of walking in the Spirit in the next chapter.[18]

---

17) Hannah Whitall Smith; *The Christian's Secret of a Happy Life;* Spire; Fleming H. Revell 1952; pgs. 98-99.

18) For further information on guidance read *Discovery*; by Ken and Alison Chant; Vision Publishing 1990.

CHAPTER FIVE

LIVING BY THE SPIRIT

"If we live by the Spirit, let us also walk by the Spirit" (Ga 5:25).

Walking in the Spirit involves walking in constant fellowship and sweet communion with the Spirit of God who lives within us, walking with God moment by moment, day after day, consistently. Many great saints of former generations had a remarkable grasp of this truth. One such was St Bernard (1090-1153). He led the Cistercian reform movement, which sought to return to a strict primitive form of Benedictine monasticism. (Benedictines had grown too soft for St. Bernard!) Though severely ascetic in his lifestyle, he was warmly romantic in his devotional writing. The following is an extract from his sermon on the Song of Songs.

> How beautiful you are among your angels, Lord Jesus,
> image of God in the day of your eternity,
> in the splendour of the saints!
> Before the morning star begotten,
> you are the glory and likeness of the Father's being,
> and the undimmed brightness of eternal life.
> How lovely you appear to me, my Lord,
> in your divine beauty!
> And yet, when you humbled yourself,

> when your unfailing light divested itself of its
> natural radiance,
> then your goodness beamed out to the wise men;
> then your love shone out more fully;
> then your grace shed its radiance more widely.
> How brightly you have risen upon me, O Star of
> Jacob;
> with what radiance you have come forth,
> O Flower of Jesse's root;
> with what gladdening light you have come to
> visit me in the darkness,
> O Dayspring from on high! [19]

Here is another shorter meditation written by the Venerable Bede (673-735). He was a monk and teacher at Jarrow in Northumbria. He played a major part in keeping alight the flame of Christian faith and learning in the Anglo Saxon Church at a time when it had been all but extinguished in much of Europe. His tomb is in the Galilee chapel in Durham Cathedral, England.

His short prayer echoes the cry of every hungry heart, searching to learn how to walk in the Spirit.

> As the thirsty deer runs to the springs of waters,
> so my spirit burns for you, loving Creator,
> and thirsts to gaze freely on you,
> the light of life.
> Oh when will it come to me, the time of love
> for which I long,
> When your face and your form are present to my
> sight. [20]

---

19) John Blakesley (Editor) ; *Paths of the Heart- Prayers of Medieval Christians*; BPCC Hazell Books, 1993; pg. 57.

20) Ibid; pg. 62.

One can feel the heart of these men who were able to spend so much of their time in contemplation and prayer, truly they knew how to walk in the presence of the Lord and they looked forward to the day they would see him face to face.

I) OBEYING DAY BY DAY

In Old Testament times Moses commanded the Israelites to practise the presence of God in their daily lives; to bring God into every aspect of living so they would not forget him. No matter what task they were performing or what trials they were undergoing, in the good times and in the bad times, they were taught to acknowledge God.

> *Hear O Israel: The Lord our God, the Lord is one. Love the Lord your God with all your heart and with all your soul and with all your strength. These commandments that I give to you today are to be upon your hearts. Impress them on your children. Talk about them when you sit at home and when you walk along the road, when you lie down and when you get up. Tie them as symbols on your hands and bind them on your foreheads. Write them on the door frames of your houses and on your gates (De 6:4-9).*

Over time the Jews developed prayers for all aspects of living. They had a prayer for when they left home to go on a journey and another for when they returned home safely. They had a prayer for when they beheld a mountain and one for when they saw a river. Another when they viewed the ocean and a beautiful sunset. They even had a prayer for new furniture!

A) THE MEANS OF GRACE

The spiritual person is one who is born of God and who follows the Lord in obedience to fulfil the requirements of Christian life and experience. These are:

Salvation: *... The word is near you; it is in your mouth and in your heart, that is, the word of faith we are proclaiming: That if you confess with your mouth, 'Jesus is Lord,' and believe in your heart that God raised him from the dead, you will be saved. For it is with your heart that you believe and are justified, and it is with your mouth that you confess and are saved* (Ro 10:8-10).

Salvation is found in no one else, for there is no other name under heaven given to men by which we must be saved (Acts 4:12).

Water baptism: *Then Jesus came from Galilee to the Jordan to be baptized by John. But John tried to deter him, saying, 'I need to be baptized by you, and do you come to me? Jesus replied, 'Let it be so now; it is proper for us to do this to fulfil all righteousness'* (Mt 3:13-15).

Repent and be baptized, every one of you, in the name of Jesus Christ for the forgiveness of your sins. And you will receive the gift of the Holy Spirit (Ac 2:38).

The baptism of the Holy Spirit: *When the day of Pentecost came, they were all together in one place. Suddenly a sound like the blowing of a violent wind came from heaven and filled the whole house where they were sitting. They saw what seemed to be tongues of fire that separated and came to rest on each of them. All of them were filled with the Holy Spirit and began to speak in other tongues as the Spirit enabled them* (Ac 2:1-4).

Reading the Word: *Faith comes from hearing the message, and the message is heard through the word of Christ* (Ro 10:17).

Let the word of Christ dwell in you richly as you teach and admonish one another with all wisdom, and as you sing psalms and hymns and spiritual songs with gratitude in your hearts to God (Cl 3:16).

Prayer: *Pray in the Spirit upon all occasions with all kinds of prayers and requests. With this in mind, be alert and always keep on praying for all the saints* (Ep 6:18).

Do not be anxious about anything, but in everything, by prayer and petition, with thanksgiving, present your requests to God (Ph 4:6).

Fellowship and Communion: *They devoted themselves to the apostles' teaching and to the fellowship, to the breaking of bread and to prayer* (Ac 2:42).

Again I tell you that if two of you on earth agree about anything you ask for, it will be done for you by my Father in heaven. For where two or three come together in my name, there am I with them (Mt 18:19-20).

Witness: *But you will receive power when the Holy Spirit comes on you; and you will be my witnesses ...* (Ac 1:8).

Be wise in the way you act toward outsiders; make the most of every opportunity. Let your conversation be always full of grace, seasoned

> *with salt, so that you may know how to answer everyone* (Cl 4:5-6).

These seven experiences are the means of grace that God has given us whereby we can learn of him and his love and fulfil the life work that he granted to us before the world was formed.

> *For we are God's workmanship, created in Christ Jesus to do good works, which God prepared in advance for us to do* (Ep 2:10).

B) FULL-TIME MINISTRY AND SECULAR WORK

Those who lead busy lives, working hard and caring for their family, feel that their Christian life would be enhanced if they could only work full-time for the Lord.

But it is no more spiritual to be in full-time ministry than it is to have a secular job. There is no line of demarcation between spiritual tasks and non-spiritual tasks. Those in leadership are to train others to do works of service. Even though you are in some form of secular work, if you have the time and the energy to undertake work for the Lord, you will find there is plenty to do (Ep 4:11-12).

At different times in our life we will have more or less time to devote to the Lord's work, depending on our home and work responsibilities. We must be careful not to neglect our primary tasks already given us by the Lord, which is to care for our loved ones.

We each have different gifts given us by the Father to assist us to complete the tasks he has given us to do. No one of these gifts is more or less spiritual than any other gift.

> *We have different gifts, according to the grace given us. If a man's gift is prophesying, let him use it in proportion to his faith. If it is serving, let him serve; if it is teaching, let him teach; if it is*

> *encouraging, let him encourage; if it is contributing to the needs of others, let him give generously; if it is leadership, let him govern diligently; if it is showing mercy, let him do it cheerfully* (Ro 12:6-8).

This text includes leadership, prophecy and teaching gifts which not all of us are called to fulfil. The other gifts listed here are gifts of serving, encouraging, contributing, and showing mercy; things we can all do as we walk in the Spirit.

These gifts are all equal in God's eyes, it is the attitude of the heart that counts with God and the development of character for which he looks. In that great day when we stand before the judgment seat of Christ there will be those who expect to be first who will be last and those who expect to be last who will be first (Mt 19:30). God looks upon the heart of man.

> *I the Lord search the heart and examine the mind, to reward a man according to his conduct; according to what his deeds deserve* (Je 17:10).

C) OUR SPIRITUAL DEVELOPMENT

There are two sides to the development of our spiritual life. We have duties to perform, and decisions to make, and God on his part helps us in all of these. What is our task? We must set ourselves apart, and commit ourselves to God's service. We must use the means of grace given us in the Word to renew our mind and to reprogram ourselves to be of greatest service. Our task is to walk in the will of God, and in the power of his Spirit.

> *Therefore I urge you brothers, in view of God's mercy, to offer your bodies as living sacrifices, holy and pleasing to God – this is your spiritual act of worship. Do not conform any longer to the pattern of this world, but be transformed by the renewing of your mind. Then you will be able to*

> *test and approve what God's will is – his good, pleasing and perfect will* (Ro 12:1-2).

What is God's task? How does he help with the development of our spiritual life? We are to work out our salvation, but God on his part works in us as well. He guides and directs us into his perfect will for our lives. As long as we are willing to be directed by the Lord and as long as we are obedient to his Word and to the promptings of the Holy Spirit then we will grow and expand in our spiritual life as Paul explains -

> *Therefore dear friends as you have always obeyed – not only in my presence, but now much more in my absence – continue to work out your salvation with fear and trembling, for it is God who works in you to will and to act according to his good purpose* (Ph 2:12-13).

How can we know our spiritual life is growing and we are walking in the Spirit? We can know because of the results that become visible in our lives. Here are some of them –

- we will practise the presence of God.
- we will pray without ceasing to God
- we will have power with God
- we will be able to persevere under pressure

1) Practising the presence of God.

Brother Lawrence, born Nicolas Herman, became a soldier at the age of eighteen, but he was wounded and had to give up this profession. For a while he became a footman until, encouraged by an uncle who was a Carmelite Friar, he offered himself as a lay brother to the Discalced Carmelites of Paris. He was accepted and given the name of Lawrence-of-the-Resurrection. His task was to buy food for the monks and to work in the kitchen. He was a humble man but so full of God that he became quite famous. He was full of the joy of God; in fact he was so aware of God and his goodness that he became filled with joy and hilarity. On some occasions he had to restrain himself from unseemly behaviour! Many came to hear his wisdom and to learn from this man of God who had learned the secret of practising the presence of God.

Here is what he had to say about practising God's presence –

> We should, he said, establish ourselves in the presence of God, talking always with him; it was an infamous thing to leave his presence to indulge in follies. We should feed our souls on high thoughts of him, and so find great joy in being with him ... We ought to give ourselves entirely to God, whether in temporal or spiritual concerns, and find our happiness in doing his will ...
>
> With (Brother Lawrence) the time of prayer was not different from any other; he had set times for it, which the Father Prior had appointed, but he neither wanted, nor asked for them, for the most absorbing work did not divert him from God. [21]

We, too, must endeavour to be aware of God at all times. Even when we are concentrating on mundane tasks our hearts can be in tune with him and, immediately our mind is free, we can return to contemplating the wonder of his presence with us, even as a compass turns automatically to the north. Indeed, when we are in tune with God, we can be growing and developing spiritually even when we are asleep, because our human spirit needs no sleep in the way our body and our mind do.

The Lord is with us always. Are we always aware of him? We will be if we are walking in the Spirit! He has promised to be with us

---

21) Brother Lawrence (translated by Donald Attwater) *The Practice of the Presence of God;* Burns and Oates; London, 1977; pgs. 30 & 37.

always, as he promised Joshua and the Israelites before they marched over Jordan and into the Promised Land –

> *"As I was with Moses, so I will be with you; I will never leave you nor forsake you"* (Jo 1:5). This is repeated for us in Hebrews 13:5, *"Never will I leave you; never will I forsake you."*

> *" ... And surely (Jesus said) I am with you always, to the very end of the age"* (Mt 28:20).

We must bring God into all our daily living; we cannot put him into some compartments of life and leave him out of others. He is interested in all we do and wants us to be aware of him at all times –

> *And whatever you do, whether in word or deed, do it all in the name of the Lord Jesus, giving thanks to God the Father through him* (Cl 3:17).

Hudson Taylor was a great apostle of God who began the China Inland Mission. Here is an extract from a book on his life and work by Phyllis Thompson: The extract comes from the very end of the book as Hudson's life was drawing to a close.

> A young missionary came to him with a query:

> You know I sometimes feel I can't bring everything to God. The big ones – yes. But many things seem too small to pray to God about. The feeling that they are too small really hinders me from praying ...

> Hudson, white haired and stocky, seemed almost surprised. 'I don't know anything about that', he said. 'Too small to pray about?'

> Some of the very small things in his life led to very big things. Giving away the last small

amount of money he had, over fifty years ago, had started him on the path of faith and obedience; the prick of a pin was so small that he scarcely noticed it, yet it had almost cost him his life: a pigtail was really a very small thing – yet how large it had loomed when he was the first and only missionary to wear one! One of the shortest prayers of his life had been when he prayed on the Brighton beach for twenty-four skilled, willing workers, but had not that prayer started the Mission for Inland China? Who could say what was big and what was not?

(He concluded) 'There is nothing small, and there is nothing great, only God is great ... We should trust him fully.' [22]

These were some of the last words Hudson spoke as he died that same evening. They illustrate how aware of God we should be and how important and necessary it is to bring God into all of our life.

The results of our being more aware of God will be:

First, a guard against temptation, and

Second, we will notice an increase in our faith as we get to know him better.

2) Praying without ceasing.

The Jews believed in one hour of preparation before they prayed and then one hour of meditation after they had completed their devotions. They took to heart the admonition in Ecclesiastes to guard their words and not to speak foolishly before God –

---

22) Phyllis Thompson; *Hudson Taylor, God's Venturer;* Moody Press, Chicago; pgs. 122-123.

> *Do not be quick with your mouth, do not be hasty in your heart to utter anything before God. God is in heaven and you are on earth, so let your words be few.* (Ec 5:2).

In Romans 12:12 and in 1 Thessalonians 5:17 we are told to be constant in prayer. So we face two facts, not only are we to be careful when we pray, but also we must be constant in our prayers. Only then can we be sure God will hear and answer our heart's cry.

We should answer these questions for ourselves before we pray a particular prayer –

- Have I been ungrateful for past answers to prayer? – Do I need to ask for forgiveness for ingratitude?

- How will I pray to God? –As Loving Father or Mighty God? How do I need to understand God for this prayer to be answered?

- Do I need comfort or do I need the Captain of my salvation with his Mighty Arm laid bare to break down strongholds?

- What is my attitude? Am I full of faith? Do I believe God can and will answer my prayer?

- Is this prayer my heartfelt prayer or is it just what I feel I should pray? – It is the heart prayer that is answered (Ps 37:4).

- What is the cost? Have I counted the cost of the answer to this prayer?

- Is this prayer asking for something that is in opposition to another prayer I have prayed? For how can God answer both prayers?

- Do I need this to be a prayer of agreement – do I need a partner in prayer?

After answering these questions to your own satisfaction and having prayed sincerely, then the time comes for listening for God's answer. This can include meditation on the Word of God, listening as he speaks through his Word, or it could just be a time of marshalling our thoughts and bringing them into order as God directs.

If you find it difficult to concentrate then have a notebook and a pen handy to write down the thoughts that come to your mind. Afterwards you can go over these carefully to see what God has shown you. There may be something that you can do for yourself to facilitate the answer to your prayer. God will not do for us what we can do for ourselves, but he will do for us what we cannot do for ourselves.

> Without God we cannot, without us God will not.
> [23]

Sometimes his answer may be, "No", sometimes it may be, "Wait", sometimes it may be, "Yes". God in his infinite wisdom knows what is best for us. Indeed he will not say, "Yes", to us if the answer would be detrimental to our salvation or draw us away from him.

But, in contrast to these more definite prayers, what does it mean to pray without ceasing? How can we pray all the time, day and night, even when we are doing our work or concentrating on other things that are important to us in life?

We can do this by having a heart attitude toward God, one that brings us immediately to think of him whenever we are not occupied with day to day situations. Our minds cannot pray constantly but our spirit can!

---

23) Quote from Augustine; Bishop of Hippo in North Africa (354-430 A.D).

Once again our spiritual compass brings us back to God each time we free our minds from other concerns. Then there are some routine tasks that do not require us to think about them and when we are doing these repetitive jobs we will find our spirit winging its way back to the Father and to the Heavenly City where we know Jesus sits on the right hand of God interceding for us constantly –

> ... *Jesus lives forever, he has a permanent priesthood. Therefore he is able to save completely those who come to God through him, because he always lives to intercede for them* (He 7:24-25).

3) Having power with God.

When we are walking in the Spirit we will always be ready to pray with someone who needs help from the Lord. Sometimes there will be spectacular results; at other times there will be no apparent result, but God will be working in the life of the person for whom we pray. Jesus promised us his authority; the authority given to him by the Father has been passed on to us (Mt 28:18). If we walk in the Spirit and are obedient to his promptings then he will lead us to those who are in need and work through us to help them through our prayers and our counsel –

> *Dear friends, if our hearts do not condemn us, we have confidence before God and receive from him anything we ask, because we obey his commands and do what pleases him. And this is his command: to believe in the name of his Son, Jesus Christ, and to love one another as he commanded us. Those who obey his commands live in him, and he in them. And this is how we know that he lives in us: we know it by the Spirit he gave us.* (1Jn 3:21-24).

Here we see the importance, if we desire to help others, of walking in the Spirit. It is because we obey his commands and seek to please him that we receive answers to our prayers. What is his command? It is that we love one another! If we do this we will live in him and he will dwell with us always. His thoughts, his will, his desires will also be ours for we will see all things from his point of view, and because of this we will pray only those prayers that he desires to answer.

4) Persevering under pressure.

If we are walking in the Spirit we will be able to persevere under pressure and stress without grumbling or complaining. The dictionary definition of 'perseverance' is the ability to keep going in God's will and against all opposition; it also means 'patience'. In all life's circumstances we do not grow, develop, and mature during times of blessing but during times of testing. If we are walking in the Spirit hard times will produce godly Christian character –

> *... We also rejoice in our sufferings, because we know that suffering produces perseverance; perseverance, character; and character, hope. And hope does not disappoint us, because God has poured out his love into our hearts by the Holy Spirit, whom he has given us* (Ro 5:3-5).

Moses cried out to God to show him his ways and we, too, can learn the ways of God if we are faithful and obedient –

> *If you are pleased with me, teach me your ways so I may know you and continue to find favour with you* (Ex 33:13).

In Psalm 103:7 we can see that God did indeed show his ways to Moses. He showed him why he did things, he explained his inner feelings to him and he listened to what Moses had to say! The children of Israel on the other hand were only allowed to see the deeds of God, the surface things he accomplished. It was not for them to understand the why of God's dealings that Moses was privileged to know. We also can be close enough to God for him to explain why he allows certain things to come into our life, though sometimes it may take many years before we see the reasons and the workings of God. In some instances we may not know or understand until we reach heaven; the wonder of this is that then, when we see Jesus in all his glory, we will have no questions. Like Job, we will say, *'Surely I spoke of things I did not understand, things to wonderful for me to know'* (Jb 42:3b).

If you want to walk in the Spirit then be prepared. Your spiritual life will be deepened and matured under pressure and testing, and as you practise God's presence and learn to pray without ceasing you will appropriate God's power and learn to persevere under any circumstance.

CHAPTER SIX

THE BATTLE FOR THE MIND

> *Therefore prepare your minds for action; be self controlled; set your hope fully on the grace to be given you when Jesus Christ is revealed* (1Pe 1:13).

Prepare your minds for action, or, as in the KJV, *'Gird up your loins'*. To gird in ancient times meant (among other things) to equip with a sword or weapon suspended from the belt, and we as Christians have been given the privilege of equipping our minds with the sword of the Spirit which is the Word of God –

> *For the word of God is living and active. Sharper than any double- edged sword, it penetrates even to dividing soul and spirit, joints and marrow; it judges the thoughts and attitudes of the heart* (He 4:12).

In the Eastern lands where they wore long flowing robes, to gird up your loins meant to pick up the robe by the hem and tuck it into the belt, thus preparing for running or for the vigorous action of battle. Our equivalent idiom would be to 'roll up our sleeves' to prepare for hard work. So here the apostle Peter is enjoining us to be prepared to strive earnestly to understand the things of God. We should never be content to drift along without studying our faith and being very sure of the things we believe, and why we believe them. We need to examine our faith so that we can explain it when called upon by others who are interested in the Christian life.

EVERY THOUGHT CAPTIVE

'Gird' also has the meaning of <u>surrounding</u> or <u>enclosing</u> a place, and in this sense we should also guard our minds from the inroads of Satan.

Johann Tauler was a Dominican friar (1300-1361). He preached to the common people of the Rhineland in their own dialect. Perhaps the most practical of all mystics, he used in his sermons homely illustrations to make simple but profound spiritual points. He has a word to say on this matter of Satanic attacks:

> The devil can bring us into all kinds of trouble. 'Oh, people say, 'if only I had a spiritual director to talk to! I get the most fearful ideas, and I am in a dreadful state.
>
> Well, my dear child, I know a lot about the ideas the devil can put in our minds, and my advice is this – what the devil puts in your mind, you put out again; be at peace. [24]

As Paul reminds us,

> *Though we live in the world, we do not wage war as the world does. The weapons we fight with are not the weapons of the world. On the contrary, they have divine power to demolish strongholds. We demolish arguments and every pretension that sets itself up against the knowledge of God, and we take captive every thought to make it obedient to Christ* (2 Co 10: 3-5).

---

24) *Eerdman's* op. cit.; pg. 36.

If you can think of your mind as a citadel, or castle, which is being attacked by Satan you will have some idea how to combat his forays. If we allow him he will try to overcome us and hammer at the door of our mind with guilt, fear, doubt, despair and misery. We must resist him as Peter warns,

> *Be self controlled and alert. Your enemy the devil prowls around like a roaring lion looking for someone to devour. Resist him, standing firm in the faith ...* (1Pe 5:8-9a).

A) BEWARE CARNALITY

Do not allow yourself to be side tracked and caught up with the things of this world, thinking about them and treasuring them above the things of God, for if you do then you will miss out on the rewards of heaven. This is illustrated well in one part of Christiana's story.

After writing the wonderful allegory of Christian's life and journey to heaven, *Pilgrim's Progress,* John Bunyan followed it with a sequel about Christiana and their children, who followed him on the pilgrimage to the Heavenly City. Because Christiana needed a helper along the way she was given a leader called Great-heart. They had many wonderful adventures before they arrived safely. At one time Great-heart showed Christiana a strange phenomenon in the house of the 'Interpreter.'

1) The Mud and the Crown.

> ... After those things had been somewhat digested by Christiana and her company, the Interpreter takes them apart again, and has them first into a room where was a man that could look no way but downwards with a muck rake in his hand. There stood also one over his head with a celestial crown in his hand, and proffered him that crown for his muck rake; but the man did

neither look up nor regard, but raked to himself the straws, the small sticks, and dust of the floor.

Then said Christiana, 'I persuade myself that I know somewhat the meaning of this; for this is the figure of a man of this world, is it not, good sir?'

'Thou hast said right,' said the Interpreter; 'and his muck rake doth show his carnal mind. And whereas thou seest him rather give heed to rake up straws and sticks, and the dust of the floor, than to do what He says that calls to him from above with the celestial crown in His hand, it is to show that heaven is but as a fable to some, and that things here are counted the only things substantial. Now, whereas it was also showed thee that the man could look no way but downwards, it is to let thee know that earthly things, when they are with power upon men's minds, quite carry their hearts away from God.'

Then said Christiana, 'O deliver me from this muck rake.' (Pr.30:8).

'That prayer,' said the Interpreter, 'has lain by till it is almost rusty: 'Give me not riches,' is scarce the prayer of one in ten thousand. Straws and sticks and dust, with most, are the great things now looked after.'

With that Christiana and Mercy wept, and said, 'It is, alas too true.' [25]

---

25) John Bunyan; *The Pilgrim's Progress*, Part II; *Christiana And Her Children*.

In this story Bunyan emphasises the futility of earthly gain, for the things of God are more substantial than anything on this earth. God's throne is more real than the natural beauty around us or than those creations of mankind we can see with the naked eye. If we are wise we will lift our eyes from the natural and consistently seek God and his righteousness. His reality is eternal and secure.

B) ABUNDANT LIFE

We should understand first of all who the enemy is. Jesus came to give us abundant life, it is Satan, the enemy of our soul, who seeks to undermine our faith –

> *The thief comes only to steal and kill and destroy; I (Jesus) have come that (you) may have life, and have it to the full* (Jn 10:10).

Jesus came to give us a life of joy and gladness; of fulfilment and peace and wonderful victory in him. Our part is simply to accept that and choose to live in that fullness (De 30:19-20).

Once you have received forgiveness and have begun to live in the rich life Christ Jesus has won for you, do not allow Satan to keep reminding you of your past mistakes. If the thought of your past sin comes back into your mind then immediately assert that the blood of Jesus has cleansed you and instead begin to think of those grand and wonderful Scriptures that thrill you when you are reading the Word of God. Such as,

> *... God did not send his Son into the world to condemn the world, but to save the world through him* (Jn 3:17).

> *For my Father's will is that everyone who looks to the Son and believes in him shall have eternal life, and I will raise him up at the last day* (Jn 6:40).

> *Therefore, there is now no condemnation for those who are in Christ Jesus, because through Christ Jesus the law of the Spirit of life set me free from the law of sin and death* (Ro 8:1).

1) Continue in the faith

Now, having fixed the foundations and learnt to choose God's way and refuse Satan's attacks, some may say, 'How do I go on to live my Christian faith?'

The answer is simple, you continue as you began, by faith! In Ro 10:9-10 we begin our Christian walk by believing in our heart and confessing with our mouth that Jesus is Lord. In this same fashion of believing and speaking out the Word we continue living out our Christian life.

> *... If you confess with your mouth, 'Jesus is Lord,' and believe in your heart that God raised him from the dead, you will be saved. For it is with your heart that you believe and are justified, and it is with your mouth that you confess and are saved.*
>
> *So then, just as you received Christ Jesus as Lord, continue to live in him* (Cl 2:6).

God is not a liar, what he says is true, so believe it, every moment of every day! For this is our victory, our faith is our victory!

> *For everyone born of God overcomes the world. This is the victory that has overcome the world, even our faith* (1 Jn 5:4).

The secret is to set your mind on the Holy Spirit, this is where you will find life and peace. You must choose to think God's thoughts about you.

The mind of sinful man is death, but the mind controlled by the Spirit is life and peace (Ro 8:6).

2) Faith, Fact and Feeling

What is faith? It is perfect trust, and confidence, believing without needing proof, just as a little child trusts his or her parent. We believe by faith and then we need to learn to live by faith. After our faith is strengthened we gain the proof of our believing by our changed feelings and emotions and by our changed lives.

First we must believe and then we receive! First faith is built up and established when the facts of Scripture are studied, after that the feelings of joy, peace and confidence in God follow. If we reverse this process, by allowing ourselves to be led by our feelings and afterwards strive to believe in the facts of God's word, then we will never have a firm foundation to build on; we will always be led by our feelings and emotions.

First believe what God has said, then after that your feelings and emotions will come into conformity with his Word. Your Christian life will be established on settled beliefs; nothing will be able to move you away from your faith.

In fact you will be able to set your face like flint to obey God no matter what happens to you; no matter what temptations come your way; no matter who tries to destroy your faith, it will remain strong because it is centred and built on the Scriptures and not on your feelings.

There are some battles to face but the remedy is there for us in the Bible.

3) The battle against fear.

Fear and faith cannot live together; fear is the enemy of faith. Some fears are good and sensible: we should fear the heat of a burning stove, or cars on the highway when we attempt to cross. These fears preserve our lives; but there are fears that are to be resisted, such as the nebulous fears and worries that plague our lives and make us anxious and afraid. God has not given us these fears, they come from our own dark imaginings or they come from Satan, who seeks to make us fearful of many things.

Sometimes these fears may stem from childhood or from some traumatic experience, but wherever they come from they need to be dealt with. We can ask God to show the cause and heal the hurt by his cleansing and delivering power –

> *For God did not give us a spirit of timidity, but a spirit of power, of love and self-discipline* (2Ti 1:7).

If we dwell on our fears they will increase, but if we dwell on our faith then that is what will grow stronger and deeper. *God's perfect love casts out all fear* (1Jn 4:18). Perfect love between us and our Father in heaven comes by getting to know him through meditation and prayer; the more time we spend with him and the more time we spend getting to know him, the more we will love and trust him.

George Muller was a great apostle of faith who supported 2,000 orphans through the prayer of faith alone (asking no money from any human source). Here he gives some guidelines concerning the way to strengthen faith:

> 1. Read the Bible and meditate upon it. God has become known to us through prayer and meditation on his own Word.

> 2. Seek to maintain an upright heart and a good conscience.

> 3. If we desire our faith to be strengthened, we should not shrink from opportunities where our faith may be tried and therefore, through trial, be strengthened.

4. The last important point for the strengthening of our faith is that we let God work for us, when the hour of trial of our faith comes, and **do not work a deliverance of our own**. Would the believer therefore have his faith strengthened, **he must give God time to work.** [26]

When we walk in the Spirit we will walk in ever-increasing faith, but as Muller warns us, we should be careful not to try to go ahead of God.

Moses did this, he was anxious to deliver his people from their slavery and he began in his own strength. The results were disastrous and he had to flee from the Egyptian authorities and spend the next forty years in the desert. Only when he had given up all thought of encompassing the deliverance of his nation was God prepared to use him.

David on the other hand was willing to wait for God's timing and he refused to usurp Saul's throne even though he had been anointed for kingship. He suffered many things because of Saul's implacable hatred but he never once took advantage of Saul even though he could have done (1 Sa 24:1-7). God honoured David's stand and eventually brought him to the throne of Israel in his own time.

4) The battle against depression

Depression can come into our lives through illness, chemical imbalance or past experiences, such as illicit sex, miscarriage, or abortion. These can cause guilt feelings and bring much sorrow and regret. Whatever the reason we must come to Jesus in prayer and ask him to cleanse us if necessary, heal us if the problem is

---

26) Basil Miller; *George Muller, Man of Faith and Miracles;* Bethany Fellowship Inc.; pgs. 58-59.

physical, and then believe that he has accomplished the work for us.

Meanwhile learn Scriptures that uplift and inspire, quote them aloud, Sing, pray in the Spirit and personalise the word of God! (To personalise Scripture means to place your name into the verse wherever it will fit). Here is an example:

> *Paul, an apostle of Christ Jesus by the will of God, to* (your name) *in* (your town), *the faithful in Christ Jesus: Grace and peace to you from God our Father and the Lord Jesus Christ. Praise be to the God and Father of our Lord Jesus Christ, who has blessed* (your name) *in the heavenly realms with every spiritual blessing in Christ. For he chose* (your name) *in him before the creation of the world to be holy and blameless in his sight" (Ep* 1:1-4).

Many years ago, in a *Guideposts* magazine, I came across the story of Midge, a woman who was hospitalised because of depression. The doctors could find no imbalance in her body chemistry, nor any reason at all why she should be in such deep depression which slowly grew worse. Over a period of ten months her husband struggled to look after their child and also maintain his work schedule; the situation was becoming desperate and many friends were praying. One day the husband was approached by two women, prayer warriors from Adriel Retreat in Lake Adriel, Pennsylvania. They felt the Lord wanted Mark to go through the imaginary putting-on of the armour of God, from Ephesians chapter six, with his wife. He had nothing to lose and much to gain, so he began to do this by telephone with her each day. As she dressed in the hospital they went through the list and slowly but surely as the days passed she began to dress herself in God's armour. After a few days she managed the task without the help of her husband. Within ten days she was completely free from depression and able to return to her family. Here is the list she worked from:

> 1. **Gird your loins with truth**. Admit that God wants you to be positive and optimistic.
>
> 2. **Strap on the breastplate of righteousness** and declare that his love and your faith will stop harmful feelings from entering your heart.
>
> 3. **Wear the gospel of peace on your feet**. Actually bend down and slip on a pair of 'shoes'. Imagine that you are standing on the Word of God and stepping out into a bright new world of mental well-being.
>
> 4. **Take up the shield of faith**. Say out loud, 'Lord, I know you will protect me from evil.'
>
> 5. **Put the helmet of salvation on your head**. Thank God in Jesus' name for protecting your mind from depression and stress.
>
> 6. **Finally, grasp the hilt of the sword of the Spirit** – which is the Word of God. Raise it high over your head, saying, 'Lord, I know this is your Word and with it I can conquer all my problems.' [27]

When we walk in the Spirit we can walk through depression to victory in Christ.

5) The battle against doubt.

Without faith it is impossible to please God, because anyone who comes to him must believe

---

[27] Guideposts Magazine, September 1983; pgs. 18-19.

that he exists and that he rewards those who earnestly seek him (He 11:6).

When doubt seizes young Christians it is a good idea for them to share this feeling with an older Christian and ask him or her for help. They can also pray and ask the Lord for reassurance, and remind themselves, first, of the miracles revealed in the Old and New Testaments and then of answers to prayer they have either seen for themselves or heard about from others.

JESSY'S STORY

During our sixteen years pastoring in Launceston, Tasmania, my husband had the privilege of bringing to the Lord an elderly lady who was crippled with arthritis. She was unable to move from her chair and became very despondent because she could do nothing for her Lord and Saviour. Jessy continually doubted God's love for her as she felt so useless. In her working life she had been a buyer for a large department store and had a strong personality and a commanding voice. Now in her declining years she felt keenly the fact that she had left her acceptance of the Lord until she was near the end of her life. There was so much she could have done for him then she thought, but now it was too late. She did not believe he could possibly love her or care for her in her crippled state. Of course we attempted to reassure her, but she kept on doubting God's love until on a particular day she broke her arm and had to go into hospital. She had to stay for some time as it was too difficult for her to be cared for at home with her arm in a sling. This was God's timing and he used it for his glory and to answer Jessy's prayers to be useful for his kingdom.

On the day, and at the moment, her Doctor announced to the nursing staff that Jessy could go home the whole ward was electrified by a loud voice coming from Jessy's bed.

'Jesus! You have come for me,' she cried. With that last cry before her death Jessy witnessed to more people than those in that hospital ward. She not only witnessed to the doctor and the nurses and to everyone nearby, but she also witnessed to the staff and patients of the whole hospital, and to the many families they belonged to, as they shared the remarkable story on their return home that evening. A friend of ours, who arrived in the ward just after Jesse's cry, felt the electrified atmosphere, as all who heard Jessy shout had to believe that she had seen Jesus; that he himself had come for her. We Christians who knew Jesse realised Jesus must have arranged the whole scene to prove his love for her; that she was a welcome newcomer to his Kingdom. This is a wonderful story and shows how the Lord is tender in his understanding of our doubts and feels for us. He can turn everything to good. No matter how black the present may seem, we have only to trust him completely. In her death Jessy witnessed to more people than she could have reached if she had been more mobile, indeed I have shared this story with many in Australia and overseas, so Jessy continues to be a witness, even though it is twenty-five years since her death.

Search the Scriptures, and study them earnestly, for in them are the words of life and victory over doubt.

6) The battle against self-pity.

Therefore strengthen your feeble arms and weak knees. Make level paths for your feet, so that the lame may not be disabled, but rather healed (He 12:12-13).

The secret path to victory over self-pity is, as in all other aspects of Christian life, to discipline your mind. Do not allow your mind to think negative destructive thoughts of sorrow, guilt or self-pity. Bring your conscious mind into subjection to your spirit and allow the Spirit of God to fill your mind with his wonder and majesty. You can control your thoughts if you make sure your memory is filled with Scripture which the Holy Spirit can then bring into your conscious mind to help you.

You can choose to indulge in thoughts of self-pity OR you can choose to think God's thoughts, the remedy is in your own mind and spirit with the help of the Holy Spirit of God. Guide your thoughts each day into positive channels, ask the Lord to direct your thoughts, and resist any evil or negative thoughts.

We are cleansed and healed by God

First, in our spirit:

> *Therefore, if anyone is in Christ, he is a new creation; the old has gone, the new has come!* (2 Co 5:17).

Second, in our mind

> *Do not be conformed any longer to the pattern of this world, but be transformed by the renewing of your mind* (Ro 12:2a).

Third, in our subconscious as the Word of God gradually penetrates to the deepest parts of our being, as Paul prays in his marvellous prayer in Ephesians chapter three –

> *I pray that out of his glorious riches he may strengthen you with power through his Spirit in your inner being, so that Christ may dwell in your hearts through faith. And I pray that you, being rooted and established in love, may have power, together with all the saints, to grasp how wide and long and high and deep is the love of Christ, and to know this love that surpasses knowledge – that you may be filled to the measure of all the fullness of God* (Ep 3:16-19).

Because of God's healing penetration into our soul and spirit our new life is safe with the Lord who watches over us and works out his purposes in us. We do our part in studying to show ourselves earnestly desiring to do God's will (2 Ti 2:15) and then he does his part in keeping us.

> *Since then you have been raised with Christ, set your hearts on things above, where Christ is seated at the right hand of God. Set your minds on things above, not on earthly things. For you died, and your life is now hidden with Christ in God. When Christ who is your life appears, then you also will appear with him in glory (Cl 3:1-4).*

7) We have plenty of power

Jesus has showered upon us his wonderful baptism of the Holy Spirit so that we have plenty of power for the battles of the Christian life (Ac 1:8). The Word has power to deliver; as we believe it and speak it out in faith, we will be victorious in Christ.

Renounce whatever seeks to gain power over you and claim your deliverance. Stand on the Word of God, by repeating the promises aloud, learning them by heart, and then accepting that the work is done. If you do this you will find it easier to walk in the Spirit; in fellowship with the Lord.

CHAPTER SEVEN

WALKING IN FREEDOM

> *I am the Lord your God, who brought you out of Egypt so that you would no longer be slaves to the Egyptians; I broke the bars of your yoke and enabled you to walk with heads held high* (Le 26:13).

Here we have a description of the Israelites being set free by God from the yoke of slavery under which the Egyptians had held them for so long. The yoke was similar to that worn by oxen and did not permit a person to hold up his head or to walk freely. This precluded the slaves from escaping easily. Unless someone could free them from the yoke they were doomed to be slaves forever.

At first, when the children of Israel walked out of Egypt, set free by the Lord through the ministry of Moses, they still had the same way of thinking and reacting that they had developed over the 400 years of their captivity. These people who had been born into slavery could not as yet think and feel as free men and women. They still had that slave mentality.

A) WHAT CAN WE LEARN FROM THIS?

1) They were not ready for war

The first thing we notice about the Israelites is that, even though they had been set free they were not prepared for war. God knew this and made provision for them

> *When Pharaoh let the people go, God did not lead them on the road through the Philistine country, though that was shorter. For God said, 'If they face war, they might change their minds and return to Egypt'. So God led the people around by the desert road toward the Red Sea...* (Ex 13:17-18a).

God knew what he was doing and even though the people were helpless in themselves he made a way for them and protected them with the pillar of fire by night and the pillar of cloud by day (14:19-20), bringing them through the Red Sea to a place of safety. Not long after this they suffered more set backs. They grew thirsty, and then hungry (15:22-25; 16:1-36) –

2) They were used to having plenty of water to drink and their food provided for them.

> *In the desert the whole community grumbled against Moses and Aaron. The Israelites said to them, 'If only we had died by the Lord's hand in Egypt! There we sat around pots of meat and ate all the food we wanted, but you have brought us out into this desert to starve this entire assembly to death* (Ex 16:2-3).

God was very patient with these people and provided for them time after time, but his patience was not inexhaustible. Eventually he rejected the generation that had a slave mentality and they perished in the desert. They could not break free from their past and spent their time complaining bitterly at the dealings of God.

3) They grumbled and complained against their leaders many times

> *The whole Israelite community set out from the desert of Sin, travelling from place to place as the Lord commanded. They camped at Rephidim,*

but there was no water for the people to drink. So they quarrelled with Moses and said, 'Give us water to drink'. Moses replied, 'Why do you quarrel with me? Why do you put the Lord to the test?' (Ex 17:1-2).

We should not feel superior to these people. If we had been there and had felt the same terrible thirst, if we had had to watch our children crying from hunger and thirst, we would have been no better than they were. Remember they had been slaves all their lives, their parents had been slaves and their grandparents, and great- great grand parents, back many generations. It was hard for them to change their thinking and to believe that freedom had really come to them. They could not see themselves as a strong and vigorous nation.

4) They were unable to see themselves as victors, strong enough to take the promised land.

Then Caleb silenced the people before Moses and said, 'We should go up and take possession of the land, for we can certainly do it.' But the men who had gone up with him said, 'We can't attack those people; they are stronger than we are' (Nu 13:30-31).

5) What does this mean for us who desire to walk in the ways of God?

As Egypt is in Scripture a 'type' of this world system, and the children of Israel are a 'type' of us Christians we can learn many things from their experiences. In this way we can avoid having their slave mentality in our Christian life.

These things happened to them (the Israelites) as examples and were written down as warnings for us, on whom the fulfilment of the ages has come.

So, if you think you are standing firm, be careful that you don't fall! (1 Co 10:11-12).

WE MUST MAKE OURSELVES FIT FOR WAR.

A) IT IS A SPIRITUAL WARFARE

Spiritual warfare for us includes prayer, gaining victory over sin and Satan, evangelism by finding and bringing others into the Kingdom of God, and conquering in the name of Jesus.

We cannot do this in our own strength but only in the strength of Jesus our Saviour. The weapons of our warfare are not worldly, they are spiritual and have divine power to tear down the strongholds of the devil and his hosts (2 Co 10:4) We have weapons, given us by the Lord, weapons and armour that we need to use (Ep 6:10-18).

In these Scriptures we see the style of warfare we must be prepared for. It is a spiritual warfare against a spiritual kingdom. It is a warfare for which we must be equipped. Paul talks of God's divine power –

1) His power is given to us freely.

I pray also that the eyes of your heart may be enlightened in order that you may know the hope to which he has called you, the riches of his glorious inheritance in the saints and his incomparably great power for us who believe. That power is like the working of his mighty strength, which he exerted in Christ when he raised him from the dead and seated him at his right hand in the heavenly realms far above all rule and authority, power and dominion, and every title that can be given, not only in the present age but also in the one to come... (Ep 1:18-20 see also 3:14-21).

The same mighty power which raised Jesus from the dead is available to us. We must meditate on this until it becomes real to us and we can believe that it is true in our lives.

2) We have weapons

In truthful speech and in the power of God; with weapons of righteousness in the right hand and in the left (2 Co 6:7).

In the Roman army of Bible times soldiers had a sword and also a shield. The shield was as high as the man himself and covered his whole body. So weapons for the right hand and the left are weapons of attack and defence; the sword of the Spirit for attack and the shield of faith for defence.

But Paul says these weapons are weapons of righteousness! We must realize that we cannot have the power of God, or be his soldiers, walking in his ways, unless we are trusting in his righteousness alone (Is 64:6).

3) We are not left powerless against Satan's attacks.

God allows us to claim the righteousness he freely gives to us through Christ our Saviour. We must rely totally on God, we dare not trust in ourselves –

God made him who had no sin to be sin for us, so that in him, we might become the righteousness of God (2 Co 5:21).

B) THE WORD OF GOD IS OUR SPIRITUAL FOOD.

1) Feed yourself.

Let the word of Christ dwell in you richly…(Cl 3:16a).

> *Do your best to present yourselves to God as one approved, a workman who does not need to be ashamed and who correctly handles the word of truth* (2 Ti 2:15).

The Israelites were used to having their food supplied to them. This provision caused a slave mentality. We must be different! Christians who expect others to do all the work of feeding them spiritually, and who only open their Bible on Sunday, not seeking to read and study the Word of God for themselves, will have this slave mentality. In direct contrast to this attitude we should fill ourselves with God's Word, and teach one another from the wisdom we learn from Scripture.

2) God's Word; your necessary food.

> *In fact, though by this time you ought to be teachers, you need someone to teach you the elementary truths of God's word all over again. You need milk, not solid food! Anyone who lives on milk, being still an infant, is not acquainted with the teaching about righteousness. But solid food is for the mature, who by constant use have trained themselves to distinguish good from evil* (He 5:12-14).

We must fill our minds with the Word of God, it must become part of our very being so that we will think with the mind of God, and so that we might be ready to teach others and lead them on to greater depths in God. God's Word is quick and powerful (He 4:12). It is truth! It will set you free. It will reshape your life. If you know it well you will naturally walk in God's will, and know how to please him.

C) WE SHOULD NOT GRUMBLE AGAINST OUR LEADERS

Obey your leaders and submit to their authority. They keep watch over you as men who must give an account. Obey them so their work will be a joy, not a burden, for that would be of no advantage to you (He 13:17).

1) Negative results

The Israelites were used to grumbling against the Egyptians and they transferred this attitude to Moses and Aaron. The results of their complaining and disobedience were disastrous for them and resulted in their ultimate destruction.

2) Positive attitude

Authority is part of the Kingdom of God, Jesus was under the authority of God and because of this he was able to lead the disciples and teach them. If we are children of God then we must show it by our willingness to be under authority. Jesus must be Lord of our lives. If we ourselves are not under authority we will be of no use to the Kingdom of God. There are too many Christians who are a law unto themselves, with no covering. They go about causing great harm to other Christians, sometimes giving personal prophecies which are spurious and cause others to make shipwreck of their lives. Protect yourself from these people, examine their life. Jesus said that we would know who was genuine by their fruit (Mt 7:16).

D) WE SHOULD SEE OURSELVES AS VICTORIOUS

1) Defeat follows disobedience.

Because of their slave mentality the Israelites missed out on the land they had been promised. Even though later on they tried to go back and repent and begin to fight it was too late, God was not with them and they failed miserably.

We should learn from their error and be careful to obey God when he speaks clearly to us, otherwise we too may miss his timing and be unable to complete the work he has planned for us.

> *Moses said, 'Why are you disobeying the Lord's command? This will not succeed! Do not go up, because the Lord is not with you. You will be defeated by your enemies' ... Nevertheless in their presumption they went up toward the high hill country ... Then the Amalekites and Canaanites who lived in that hill country came down and attacked them and beat them down all the way to Hormah* (Nu 14:39-45).

2) Watch and pray

What great sadness it is in these days to see once-great ministries laid aside because they have let some sin overcome them.

> *Therefore I do not run like a man running aimlessly; I do not fight like a man beating the air. No, I beat my body and make it my slave so that after I have preached to others, I myself will not be disqualified for the prize* (1 Co 9:26-27).

3) Live victoriously

We must be careful then to see ourselves as victorious, ready to do God's will and to follow in the steps of Jesus. We have been given the power to become God's children, we have been given the power to live victoriously. That same power that raised Jesus from the dead dwells in us. We must look to Jesus, the Author and Finisher of our faith, dwelling in his strength and not in our own inabilities and weaknesses.

> *This is love for God: to obey his commands. And his commands are not burdensome, for everyone born of God overcomes the world. This is the victory that has overcome the world, even our faith* (1 Jn 5:3-4).

To gain that victory, truly to learn to walk in the Spirit, means we must break free from the spirit of slavery; break free of a slave mentality.

> *For you did not receive a spirit that makes you a slave again to fear, but you received the spirit of sonship. And by him we cry, 'Abba, Father.' The Spirit himself testifies with our spirit that we are God's children* (Ro 8:15-16).

4) Guard against fear

Fear is the thing we must guard against, for it can cause us to slip back into this spirit of slavery. However, we can overcome fear through our faith in Jesus; we need no longer be afraid. Fear is overcome by faith. As we dwell in the shadow of our Almighty God we can live a new life of victory in him. We can have victory over sin, over sickness, over all the harmful experiences of the past.

5) Love casts out fear!

> *There is no fear in love. But perfect love drives out fear, because fear has to do with punishment. The one who fears is not made perfect in love* (1 Jn 4:18).

Our love and trust in the Lord delivers us from fear, for we know we are safe from punishment. Christ has borne our sin on the cross and we do not need to be afraid of God, but can love and trust him as a child loves and trusts its parent.

Let us look again at our text in Leviticus:

> *I am the Lord your God who brought you out of Egypt ...*

Here God reminds Israel that he is the Mighty God, the God of the covenants, he has proved his power; they can measure his power by his deeds. He has brought them out, and set them free, which they could not do themselves, and neither can we; our salvation comes from God and from him alone.

> *...so that you would no longer be slaves to the Egyptians.*

By faith we are saved, by faith we are set free from sin, we are no longer the slaves of sin; we have the power of choice. We can choose to serve God!

> *I broke the bars of your yoke ...*

The yoke of Satan was binding us but God has broken that yoke. We are now free from sin, we can choose not to sin. We are now free from sickness, we can claim health. We are now free from bad memories, God is able to set us free from all those thoughts that bind and enslave us. We are now free to forgive as God has forgiven us, to be set free from anything that would keep us from loving and serving God as he wants us to.

> *...and enabled you to walk with heads held high*

God came to give us back our dignity, to raise us up and make us part of his family, part of his army, we are special to him no matter how ordinary we feel. We have been given authority to go out and live for him, a life of obedience, a life of victory; a life of service; a wonderfully full life; an exciting life for God.

> God calls ordinary men and women and makes them extraordinary. God does not see you as you see yourself, he does not see you as others see you. God sees you as you can become when you

are anointed and endued with spiritual power. God uses ordinary people. [28]

In our next chapter we learn more of our victory in Christ.

---

28) Pat Hulsey; *Power Principles*; Harvest International Institute.

CHAPTER EIGHT

BUILDING IN THE SPIRIT

> *If you remain in me and my words remain in you, ask whatever you wish, and it will be given you. This is to my Father's glory, that you bear much fruit, showing yourselves to be my disciples* (Jn 15:7-8).

I) LIVING IN THE WORD

Abiding in Christ occurs naturally as we allow his Word to dwell in us. When the Word of God lives in us abundantly we learn the wisdom and understanding we need to walk with him.

> *Let the word of Christ dwell in you richly as you teach and admonish one another with all wisdom* ... ((Cl 3:16a).

The Word must become a part of our very being, interwoven with our mind and memory. In this way our spirit becomes recreated and renewed by the Word and by our faith in the Word. As we learn and receive revelation a marvellous thing begins to happen; our minds are cleansed and we no longer have room for negative or sinful thoughts (Ep 5:25-27).

God has given to us the means for victory in our Christian life (1 Jn 1:8-9). Forgiveness comes immediately when we repent and confess our failures. In the meantime cleansing from unrighteousness progresses at deeper and deeper levels over time and gradually we lose the desire to sin; we learn to choose life and not death (De 30:19).

The Holy Spirit has promised to bring Scripture to our minds when we need it (Jn 14:26). Satan however endeavours to whisper evil thoughts to us and we must be careful not to allow these evil or negative thoughts to dwell in our minds. Immediately the wicked thought comes we should breathe a prayer to the Father and replace that thought with a positive key Scripture like this one,

> *Rejoice in the Lord always. I will say it again: Rejoice! Let your gentleness be evident to all. The Lord is near* (Ph 4:4).

A) VICTORY IN CHRIST

Do not allow Satan to rob you of your victory in Christ by making you feel guilty for random trigger thoughts. These thoughts lead on to other thoughts that cause you to spiral downward into despair as you remember the sins of the past. If you allow or indulge these thoughts they can lead on to depression and a feeling of failure. Replace them with Scriptures of Christ's victory over Satan and all his works, and continue to live on for the Lord. Use Scriptures like these –

> *(Jesus replied) I saw Satan fall like lightening from heaven. I have given you authority to trample on snakes and scorpions and to overcome all the power of the enemy; nothing will harm you* (Lu 10:18).

> *... That power is like the working of his mighty strength, which he exerted in Christ when he raised him from the dead and seated him at his right hand in the heavenly realms, far above all rule and authority, power and dominion, and every title that can be given, not only in the*

present age but also in the one to come (Ep 1:19-21).

Read, memorise and meditate in Scripture so earnestly that there remains no room for Satan to gain a foothold in your life. Be like Jesus in this so that Satan will have no hold over you (Jn 14:30).

1) Your sins are forgiven.

If you are a child of God then your past has been dealt with, your sins are forgiven, there is no longer any need for you to dwell on the past. Instead look forward to the future while learning the Word of God and discovering the ways of God.

Trust in God as you continue to store messages of faith and victory in your mind, then you will lead a life that is worthy of the Lord and fully pleasing to him (Cl 1:10).

2) A secret we must learn.

To lead a life of victory we must abide in the Lord while leaving our fruitfulness to him. He is the gardener, he does the pruning and cultivating; we cannot do this for ourselves. The fruit that grows on a grape-vine does not struggle to grow, it just comes into existence naturally as the orchardist cultivates it and provides it with the nourishment it needs (Jn 15:1-4).

We cannot do God's gardening work for him, this only results in frustration on our part. The harder we try the more abysmally we fail, the victory flees from us and we sink into depression, and Paul explains this to us so eloquently in Romans chapter seven.

Our part is to abide in Jesus, we are a branch and we draw our life from him. He is the vine, the one who feeds us with the life-giving sap of the Word we read and store in our minds. As the gardener, he prunes us and encourages us to bear fruit. This fruit is a natural happening, it occurs with no effort on our part. Jesus has won the victory for us on the cross.

> *Therefore, there is now no condemnation for those who are in Christ Jesus, because through Christ Jesus the law of the Spirit of life set me free from the law of sin and death* (Ro 8:1-2).

We bring glory to God by allowing him to produce the fruit in us and through us. Once we come to this place of rest then we can begin to follow the Lord's leading for our life, discovering the work he has for us to do.

3) There is a balance.

In Colossians 3:5, 8, 12 & 14 we discover there is a putting to death; a ridding of ourselves from sin and a clothing of ourselves with the fruit of the Spirit.

'But', you might say, 'Isn't this doing something for myself?'

Not if you look at in this way; the putting to death, and the reclothing of ourselves with godly attributes is accomplished by the decisions we make day by day.

We must be aware that there is a balanced walk for us between abiding and doing. This prevents us from falling from liberty into license; from the freedom to live and walk in Christ while seeking to do his will, and the bondage of falling into sin. This thinking comes from a wrong understanding that God will forgive us no matter what we do.

No! Whoever claims to live in Christ must prove it by obeying his commands and walking through life as he did while he was with us in the flesh.

> *But if anyone obeys his word, God's love is truly made complete in him. This is how we know we are in him: whoever claims to live in him must walk as Jesus did* (1Jn 2:5b-6).

So, in effect our Christian life consists of abiding in Christ and deciding each time we are tempted that we will follow his way and not the way of selfishness or sin. When we reach this understanding we discover the power of God to deliver us from bondage.

4) We discover we have the power to resist sin.

Before we were born again we had little power to say 'No!' to Satan's temptations. After we begin to abide in Jesus we find we do have the strength to resist.

Satan no longer has power over us, we are set free from the curse of sin, for God sets his axe to the root of sin in our lives and not just to the visible fruit of our sin. We have a double cure in the cross of Jesus, from the fruit and the root of sin.

Life then becomes a series of decisions. We draw nourishment from the vine (Jesus) through the power of the Holy Spirit, and as each decision comes along we decide to go God's way, the way of life and hope and everlasting joy!

We have no strength in ourselves, all of our strength comes from our connection to the Saviour. We are strengthened with all power to overcome (1 Co 10:13). Now we are ready to participate in the very nature of Christ.

II) BUILDING THE MIND OF CHRIST

> *... His divine power has given us everything we need for life and godliness through our knowledge of him who called us by his own glory and goodness ... make every effort to add to your faith goodness; and to goodness, knowledge; and to knowledge, self control; and to self control, perseverance; and to perseverance, godliness; and to godliness, brotherly kindness; and to brotherly kindness, love. For if you possess these*

> *qualities in increasing measure, they will keep you from being ineffective and unproductive in your knowledge of our Lord Jesus Christ (2 Pe 1:3 & 5-8).*

Christian life and character consist of the essential building blocks discussed here and we are urged to develop them in our life. If we do then we will be effective and productive in our knowledge of Jesus our Lord.

FAITH – *(Gr. 'pistis'* - a firm conviction)

This is a good foundation stone to begin with; this kind of faith is a firm conviction, producing a full acknowledgement of God's revelation and truth (Ac 4;12). There is no other name but the name of Jesus to save us and bring us into God's kingdom. We grow in faith as we study Scripture and enrich our minds with God's revelation of the new birth We must begin here, our first building block toward the nature of Christ.

GOODNESS OR VIRTUE – *(Gr. 'arete' – moral excellence)*

The essential goodness of Jesus has its foundation in moral excellence. No sin was found in him, he is pure and holy. We must cling to his righteousness and despise our own feeble attempts to claim any goodness. If we do try to claim our own righteousness then we are told it is as filthy rags in God's sight (Is 64:6).

KNOWLEDGE – *(Gr. 'gnosis' – working knowledge)*

This kind of knowledge is working knowledge, the kind of knowledge that an architect needs to read the plans for a building or an engineer needs to understand the plans for a bridge. We as Christians need a working knowledge of Scripture and the principles of God. The writer of Hebrews illustrates this in 5:11b-14.

> *... you are slow to learn. In fact, though by this time you ought to be teachers, you need someone*

> *to teach you the elementary thoughts of God's word all over again. You need milk, not solid food! Anyone who lives on milk, being still an infant, is not acquainted with the teaching about righteousness. But solid food is for the mature, who by <u>constant use</u> have trained themselves to distinguish good from evil.*

Note the words, 'constant use', as we study and meditate on the Scriptures we move from immature to mature, we no longer need to be fed but we are ready to feed others.

The book, *Fresh Manna,* by Stan DeKoven would be an excellent beginning to learning and understanding ways of studying the Bible. [29]

SELF-CONTROL – *(Gr. 'enkrates'* – temperate)

This self control is needed to resist temptation when it comes to us. The sting can be taken from temptation if we pre-decide, before the temptation comes that there are some things we will never do, certain stands we will always take, such as against adultery, divorce, and abortion. We cannot have complete self-control without the help of the Holy Spirit, but if we cry out to him he will help us (1Co 10:13).

PERSEVERANCE – *(Gr. 'hupomone'* – patient endurance)

This kind of perseverance is shown when people who are suffering show patience, bearing trials calmly and without complaint. They endure, showing they have the ability to withstand hardship, adversity and stress. A short sharp martyrdom with a quick death would be less hard to bear than many years of constant suffering. The saints Peter was writing to were suffering the confiscation of their goods, imprisonment and many times, death in the arena.

---

29) Stan DeKoven; *Fresh Manna;* Vision Publishing. 1990.

These things are happening again in our day. Once again people are being called upon to die for their faith, and they too need to persevere with patient endurance. We who live in present safety should not forget them but lift them up in prayer for their faith to be strengthened.

GODLINESS– *(Gr. 'eusebeia'* – to be devout)

Godliness illustrates the kind of piety that seeks to please God (Ep 5:8-10; Ex 33:13,17; 1 Jn 3:21). It refers to those who have built a proper foundation for godliness to flourish in their lives. There are many Scriptures that enjoin us to please God. *"Find out what pleases the Lord,"* Paul tells us in Ephesians, and we should seek to know what it is that gives the Lord satisfaction.

BROTHERLY AFFECTION– *(Gr. 'philadelphia'* – brotherly love)

This is the kind of love we should have for the members of the body of Christ with whom we worship. We should seek to help one another and show by our concern that we care. (Ja 5:16).

LOVE– *(Gr. 'agape'* – benevolence, goodwill, charity, generosity)

This is the love that comes from God and it is the kind of love we should have for those outside the fellowship, those who have not yet received Christ as Saviour.

These last two loves are the result of all that has been built up before them, they are the crown of our character in Christ, and also the foundation.

GAINING MATURITY

Nothing is more necessary to Christian growth than a good self-image in Christ. With an excellent self-image comes a sense of belonging, of being loved. Deep hurts can be healed when we know we are precious to God. We should let the reality of God's love become more real to us than any earthly love.

> *The Lord your God is with you, he is mighty to save. He will take great delight in you, he will quiet you with his love, he will rejoice over you with singing* (Zep 3:17).

The second thing that comes with a good self-image is a sense of worth and value, the feeling that I count and I have something to contribute. Once again, we gain this from God's love for us.

> *For God so loved the world that he gave his one and only Son, that whoever believes in him shall not perish but have eternal life* (Jn 3:16).

The third and last result of a good self-image is a sense of being competent, the understanding that I can cope, there is nothing that God and I can't handle!

> *I can do everything through him who gives me strength* (Ph 4:13).

If we possess this healthy Christian self-image then we can go on to walk in the Spirit, building a godly character, standing mature in Christ, able to influence others for good.

CHAPTER NINE

WALKING THROUGH TRIALS

For four years John Newton (1725-1807) was a profligate English sea captain who traded and transported slaves. He left the sea in 1755, was converted to Christ and became an Anglican priest in 1764. Newton is famous for writing the marvellous and well-loved hymn, *Amazing Grace*. Here he likens the Christian life to a sea voyage and in doing so shows his eloquence, and his knowledge of the sea and ships:

> My connections with sea-affairs have often led me to think, that the varieties observable in Christian experience may be properly illustrated from the circumstances of a voyage. Imagine to yourself a number of vessels, at different times, and from different places, bound to the same port; there are some things in which all these would agree – the compass to steer by, the port in view, the general views of navigation, both as to the management of the vessel and determining their astronomical observations, would be the same in all. In other respects they would differ; perhaps no two of them would meet with the same distribution of winds and weather. Some we see set out with a prosperous gale; and when they almost think their passage secured they are checked by adverse blasts; and, after enduring

much hardship and danger, and frequent expectations of shipwreck, they just escape, and reach the desired haven. Others meet the greatest difficulties at first; they put forth in a storm, and are often beaten back; at length their voyage proves favourable, and they enter the port with a rich and abundant entrance. Some are hard beset with cruisers and enemies, and obliged to fight their way through; others meet with little remarkable in their passage.

Is it not thus in the spiritual life? All true believers walk by the same rule, and mind the same things; the word of God is their compass; Jesus is both their polar star and their sun of righteousness; their hearts and faces are all set Zion-ward. Thus far they are as one body animated by one Spirit; yet their experience, formed upon these common principles, is far from being uniform. The Lord in his first call, and in his following dispensations, has a regard to the situation, temper and talents of each, and to the particular services or trials he has appointed them for. Though all are exercised at times, yet some pass through the voyage of life much more smoothly than others. But he, *"who walks upon the wings of the wind, and measures the waters in the hollow of his hand,"* (Ps 18:10; Is 40:12) will not suffer any of whom he has once taken charge to perish in the storms, though for a season perhaps, many of them are ready to give up all hopes.[30]

---

30) Richard Cecil; *The Life of John Newton;* Baker Book House; Grand Rapids, Michigan. 1981; pgs. 94-96.

MANIFOLD TRIALS

> *In this you greatly rejoice, though now for a little while you may have had to suffer grief in all kinds of trials. These have come so that your faith – of greater worth than gold, which perishes even though refined by fire – may be proved genuine and may result in praise glory and honour when Jesus Christ is revealed* (1 Pe 1:6-7).

We have a living hope and an inheritance that can never perish or fade away, kept in heaven for us. We rejoice in this even though during this life we suffer many trials. They are allowed by the Lord for a special reason, to test us and prove that our faith is genuine.

Our trials are intended to purify us, and to see how closely bonded we are to Christ. From the beginning this has always been God's method.

In our text Peter talks about 'all kinds of (manifold) trials,' (Gr *poikilos* – 'many coloured' or 'varied') – so our trials can take many forms, sometimes we may not even realise we are being tested until after the trial is over. It is only in looking back that we can see how God was testing us, checking that our faith is secure in him and that we have a steadfast resolve to follow him, no matter what happens (1 Pe 1:3-9).

The trials of our Christian life come between 'glories'. These are mountain-top experiences of blessing that are bestowed on us to give us comfort, and the energy and courage to continue our pilgrimage. The valleys of our life, the trials and troubles that we must all face, are periods when we are changed and refined by the Holy Spirit. During these testing times God is with us as he promised, though we cannot always sense his presence.

God does not send these times of trial. But when they do come, God uses them to bring about the changes we need to become more like Jesus. As in Old Testament times God has his reasons for allowing testing, as Moses revealed to the Israelites toward the end of their wilderness experience –

> *And you shall remember all the way which the Lord your God has led you these forty years in the wilderness, that he might humble you, testing you to know what was in your heart, whether you would keep his commands or not* (De 8:2).

As in the physical sense a body does not grow and develop muscle when it has no exercise, so in the spiritual we do not grow and develop during times of blessing but only during times of testing. Trials produce Christian character, the fruit of the Spirit. These are listed in Galatians 5:22-23 as love, joy, peace, kindness, goodness, patience, faithfulness, gentleness, and self-control.

There is no doubt that testing times produce strong character if they are faced with courage, fortitude and a mature attitude.

Our trials also humble us and give us a hunger for the manna of heaven, the Word of God. The genuine Christian who is suffering some trial, some sorrow, will reach out to the Word of God, searching for an answer to his or her suffering, for some comfort from the Lord, and God will always feed the hungry heart and, with his heavenly manna, inject life into the grieving soul.

There are many reasons why we can endure these trials with joy in our hearts:

First there is the hunger we gain for the Word of life as shown in Deuteronomy 8:3.

> *He humbled you causing you to hunger and then feeding you with manna, which neither you nor your fathers had known, to teach you that man does not live on bread alone but on every word that comes from the mouth of the Lord.*

Second our faith is tested by fire and our faith to overcome will bring us praise and honour from our Lord when he comes –

> *So that the genuineness of your faith, more precious than gold which though perishable is tested by fire, may redound to praise and glory and honour at the revelation of the Lord Jesus Christ* (1 Pe 1:7).

Third we are laying up treasure in heaven, an eternal glory that puts our trials into their right perspective –

> *For our light and momentary troubles are achieving for us an eternal glory that far outweighs them all* (2 Co 4:17).

Our faith is tested, strengthened and proved genuine by our trials; we are fed by the Lord with his precious words of love and caring, and our overcoming faith will result in praise, glory and honour in that day when Jesus comes.

A) ESTABLISHED AND STRENGTHENED

The following list is taken from William Barclay's NT Commentary.[31]

> *And the God of all grace, who hath called us unto his eternal glory by Christ Jesus, after that ye have suffered awhile, make you perfect, stablish, strengthen, settle you* (1 Pe 5:10 KJV).

1) Through our suffering God will perfect us. (Gr. *'katartizo'*,– 'perfect' means 'setting a fracture'). It is used in Mark 1:19 for mending fishing nets. It means to supply that which is missing, to mend that which is broken, to restore that which is

---

31) William Barclay; *The Daily Study Bible*; James and Peter; St. Andrew Press. Edinburgh. 1963; pgs. 323-324.

lacking or wanting. So suffering, if it is accepted in humility and love can add to our character what may be lacking.

2) Through our suffering God will establish us. (Gr.'s*terizo'*– 'establish' means making something 'firm and as solid as granite'). Suffering does one of two things to a person, either they collapse into bitterness or they gain a solidity of character which they could not gain otherwise. Like an athlete who trains until his whole body is toughened and he has enormous staying power, his muscles become as though tempered steel.

3) Through our suffering God will strengthen us. (Gr. *'sthenoo'*– 'strengthen' means 'fill with strength'). It is true that the life that has no discipline or effort becomes a flabby life. On the contrary our life must be tried in the furnace of trial and crisis. The wind that would extinguish a weak flame, will instead fan a stronger flame to a greater blaze. In the same way God uses our trials to strengthen us and make us stronger.

4) Through our suffering God will settle us. (Gr. *'tithemi'* – 'settle' means 'to lay a foundation'). It is only when we suffer that we are driven to the bedrock of our faith, there we find what cannot be shaken; we find the difference between essentials and non-essentials in our life. When experiencing grief some things, which in the past seemed so important, seem now of little if any importance.

Suffering then can drive us to bitterness and despair or it can perfect, establish, strengthen and settle us and take us on to God's eternal glory.

B) SUFFERING PRODUCES CHARACTER

Therefore since we have been justified through faith, we have peace with God through our Lord Jesus Christ, through whom we have gained access by faith into this grace in which we now stand. And we rejoice in the hope of the glory of

> *God. Not only so, but we also rejoice in our sufferings, because we know that suffering produces perseverance; perseverance character; and character hope. And hope does not disappoint us, because God has poured out his love into our hearts by the Holy Spirit, whom he has given us* (Ro 5:1-4).

Here we see that suffering produces perseverance, character and hope. In the word 'perseverance' we catch a glimpse of what it means to keep going under pressure, no matter what the circumstances, no matter what we are going through. Perseverance' means 'to be steadfast'. We must keep our eyes fixed on Jesus and the heavenly rewards waiting for us in that great day when we will hear Christ say,

> *"Well done good and faithful servant"* (Mt 25:21).

The result of our perseverance and the building of our Christian character is hope. From the Gr. *elpis* the word 'hope' means 'the happy anticipation of good'. Our fond and glad hope is for our ultimate salvation and entrance into heaven. Everyone must have hope for the future, this is what keeps us advancing and going on with God. This is what gives us the security of our heavenly reward. Knowing that it is waiting for us above keeps us stable with our eyes firmly fixed on the Lord. Hope helps us to continue on no matter what trial, or sorrow, or hard times we may go through. Hope for the future is an essential part of our Christian experience and stability in Christ.

During the times of crisis and trial what we have gained in God is tested under fire. As we have only what we hold under pressure we soon discover exactly how strong we are in God, how much perseverance we have, how strong our character is, and how effervescent is our hope in Christ.

As we go through these times of trial we are enlarged and prepared to assist and comfort others. We are driven to prayer, to search through the Scriptures, to find answers, to understand principles and to claim promises (Ps 4:1).

When we have worked through these and made them our own we can use what we have learned to teach others.

1) The God of comfort.

For instance, we pray for comfort and God answers our prayer by showing us 2 Corinthians 1:3-4 –

> *Praise be to the God and Father of our Lord Jesus Christ, the Father of compassion and the God of all comfort, who comforts us in all our troubles, so that we can comfort those in any trouble with the comfort we ourselves have received from God.*

We pray for enlargement and a deepening of our character and God leads us to Psalm 4:1 (KJV) -

> *Answer me when I call, O God of my right. Thou hast enlarged me when I was in distress.*

So we begin to see that our sufferings, our trials, may have some use after all. They not only assist us to grow as we rely on the Lord to make sense of our troubles, but we learn wisdom and the ways of God. We can then use the wisdom God has taught us to assist others who may find themselves in similar troubles. God does not waste any experience of ours that can be used for his ultimate glory!

2) Principles of maturity and dependence.

Sometimes God works to delay an answer to prayer. Why does he do this? It is because he works by the principle of maturity. He wants us to grow spiritually into fully mature adults just as any father desires of his children.

Why must we suffer trials? We have seen already that if we cling to the Lord and trust him to bring us through, if we persevere, refusing to give up no matter what happens, then our character is strengthened, and our hearts are enlarged. We are then filled with compassion and wisdom to help and assist others who may be struggling in deep waters.

There is something even more important that occurs during our periods of suffering and trial. **In them we are broken enough to become completely dependent upon God**, all our human pride and self-sufficiency is swallowed up.

> *Brothers, think of what you were when you were called. Not many of you were wise by human standards; not many were influential; not many were of noble birth. But God chose the foolish things of the world to shame the wise; God chose the weak things of the world to shame the strong. He chose the lowly things of the world and the despised things – and the things that are not – to nullify the things that are, so that no one may boast before him* (1 Co 1:26-31).

A trial or crisis does not tell us what we have, but what we do not have. It reveals our weaknesses and just how much we need the Lord. And then too, it is not so much what happens during our trial but our reaction to what happens that is significant. This too determines our growth in the spiritual life.

Are your reactions bitter, or are they trustful and pure before the Lord?

3) Joseph's trials

Joseph was chosen for a special task and he endured many trials while God was working out his purposes in his life. You can read the story in Genesis chapters 37-47.

Like Joseph, in a sense we are all 'special' to God, and we each have our own task to complete in life, a task that the Lord has ordained in advance for each of us (Ep 2:10). We are also called to be 'letters' known and read by everybody (2 Co 3:2-3).

In his early life Joseph was given the blessing of two dreams of future triumph to keep him going throughout his trials. Many times he must have pondered and wondered why he was suffering through thirteen long years.

We too have been given a blessing of baptism in the Holy Spirit and a promise of future victory to empower us for God and to comfort us as we go through the times when we do not understand why we are suffering.

Joseph bore his trials bravely, and his reactions were good. First he resisted sin through Potiphar's wife (Ge 39:7) and then he resisted bitterness during the time he was forgotten by Pharoah's butler, the man who left him languishing in prison for a further two years (Ge 41:1).

There are three different reactions Christians can have when they are going through trials–

- **A childish reaction** – complaining and bitter.

- **A more mature reaction** – I don't understand this, please help me to understand and grow because of this trial.

- **A fully mature reaction** – rising up in faith, grasping hold of the promises. Not passive but positive, searching for answers, making the promises of God work by the exercise of faith.

God allowed the trials in Joseph's life to preserve his family from famine many years later. Seventeen when he was sold into slavery,

Joseph was thirty when Pharaoh raised him up to rule Egypt (Ge 41:46). During this period of time God changed Joseph from a spoiled favourite son to a wise ruler and administrator.

His training in Potiphar's house and later on in the jail were just what he needed to give him the expertise to administer the successful preparations for the preservation of the Egyptian people throughout the famine, which had been foretold by Pharaoh's dreams.

Beware: sometimes when we go through adversity we can be extremely Christlike and do and say all of the right things, but then when prosperity comes, and suddenly we are lifted into a position of trust, we can fail because pride creeps in. Joseph did not fail, but kept a good attitude throughout the whole period, first of oppression and then of triumph.

- He held no grudges against his brothers, though he did test them and found them changed in their attitude.
- He allowed no bitterness to influence the way he treated his family.
- He forgave his brothers freely.
- He shared his good fortune.

His own brothers threw Joseph into the pit. His own master threw him in gaol. The man he befriended left him in prison. It is true therefore that we too can sometimes suffer through our own family, or close friends; even through people we love.

Through it all Joseph's attitude remained good and he comes down to us as a type of Christ. No sin is recorded in the Bible against his life and in many ways his life portrayed in 'type' the Christ who was to come. Through the story of Joseph we are encouraged to be strong persons in Christ. Your testing times become stepping stones toward a Christlike character so that you can inspire and influence others.

Remember to keep your trials in perspective; think of the glory to come! God uses times of suffering to refine us, to empty us of self, to teach us to rely totally and completely on him. No flesh should glory in his presence. To him belongs the glory, all of the glory.

CHAPTER TEN

WALKING IN FAMILY LIFE

How can we please God in our family life? How can we walk in the Spirit through the years of marriage and family life, loving our spouse and nurturing and bringing up our children in the love of the Lord? And how can we show God's perfection in our church family?

In Proverbs 6:16-19 we read of the seven things God hates. We can extrapolate from this that there must be seven things God loves to see in our family and church life; seven principles that please him and give him joy and delight –

> *There are six things the Lord hates, Yes, seven that an abomination to him: a proud look, a lying tongue, hands that shed innocent blood, a heart that devises wicked plans, feet that are swift in running to evil, a false witness who speaks lies and one who sows discord among brethren (NKJV).*

A) FIRST PRINCIPLE: HUMILITY

If God hates a proud look then he loves a person who is humble, not proud.

Indeed he tells us this in 1 Pe 5:5b-6 –

> *God opposes the proud but gives grace to the humble. Humble yourselves therefore under God's mighty hand, that he may lift you up in due time.*

C. S. Lewis had this to say about pride during one of his BBC broadcasts during the war years:

> "It was through pride that the devil became the devil: Pride leads to every other vice: it is the complete anti-God state of mind ... How is it that people who are quite obviously eaten up with pride can say they believe in God and appear to themselves to be very religious? I'm afraid it means they are worshipping an imaginary God ... If anyone would like to acquire humility, I can, I think, tell him the first step. The first step is to realise that one is proud. And a biggish step, too. At least, nothing can be done before it. If you think you're not conceited, it means you are very conceited indeed." [32]

Pride can cause great harm in family life, the refusal to say, "I'm sorry", the refusal to apologise or admit wrong, is devastating to a marriage. Pride is upsetting also to any children in the family, because parents who never admit fault do not give their child permission to make mistakes.

But if a parent is not too proud to say, "I was wrong," then the child can also relax and admit when he is wrong. Paul tells us in Ep 6:4, *'Provoke not your children to anger'* (don't exasperate your children).

Pride builds walls around us and keeps us from loving as we should, but humility keeps us soft and gentle and easy to approach. So instead of haughty, proud looks, God loves humility and meekness.

---

32) C. S. Lewis (Excerpts) *Christian Behaviour;* Centenary Press London; 1943; pgs. 46-47.

> *Moses was a very humble man, more humble than anyone else on the face of the earth* (Nu 12:3).

Moses was meek, but he was not weak, he learned leadership in the desert and became a strong leader, accomplishing great things for God. He led the children of Israel out of Egypt through God's mighty hand. We can read of the extraordinary acts of God in the book of Exodus.

He did not defend himself when Aaron and Miriam challenged his authority (Nu 12:1-15), nor when Korah, Dathan and Abiram also challenged him (Nu 16:1-35). Rather he let God deal with those who opposed his leadership.

How did his meekness show itself? He did not defend himself, and he made himself a servant to his people (Nu 11:14) and he was willing for his name to be blotted out if that was necessary to preserve them (Ex 32:32). *'Humble yourselves before the Lord and he will lift you up'*, is the admonishment from James (4:10).

We should display this same meekness, not defending nor justifying ourselves; indeed, true maturity does not need to justify itself. Those who walk in the Spirit will walk in humility.

In a family setting meekness will ask, "How can I bring happiness to my loved ones?" Giving happiness, not taking it; proving love by service; thus setting an excellent example, these things should be our aim.

In our church family too we should do away with pride, learning true Christianity, growing in humility and strength in Christ and dedicating ourselves to a life of service for God, helping those who are in any need (Mt 25:31-46).

> *Who is wise and understanding among you? Let him show it by his good life, by deeds done in the humility that comes from wisdom* (Ja 3: 13).

B) SECOND PRINCIPLE: TRUTH

If God hates a lying tongue then he loves a person who lives in, and speaks, the truth.

> *Do not lie to each other, since you have taken off your old self with its practices and have put on the new self, which is being renewed in knowledge in the image of its Creator* (Cl 3:9-10).

How do we lie? Perhaps many times unintentionally, not intending to deceive, but instead wanting to appear at our best for our loved ones.

During an engagement period it is very important we do not pretend to be something we are not merely to please the one we love and want to marry. Instead many questions should be asked of one another before marriage. Courting should be a time of exploring one another and of discovering opinions on the various details of what it takes to make a good marriage.

It is hypocritical to seek to be acceptable by hiding character traits. Some temperaments clash, some fit together, and we should seek to be wise in our understanding of one another before we take the irrevocable step of marriage.

Do not deceive yourself by saying, "I will change him/her after marriage." It won't happen! Listen to the way they speak to their parents, brothers, sisters, because that is the way they will speak to *you* after marriage.

Instead the Lord wants you to speak and live in truth, as he admonishes us through Paul –

> *Stand firm with the belt of truth buckled around your waist* (Ep 6:14).

It is hard work, living a lie. One needs a good memory for sooner or later the truth will out! So be honest and straight forward with each other.

However, do not use this principle to pick fault with one another in the mistaken belief that you should be truthful and open, no matter how much your words hurt. Remember the beam in your own eye (Mt 7:3-5). When you notice a fault in someone else it is possible the same fault lies in you.

On the other hand don't let walls grow up between you; seek to keep open communication with each other in marriage, learn to be diplomatic; it is possible to discuss problems without attacking and hurting one another.

Does this mean I have to tell my spouse every little thing? No, I do not believe so.

> *Only the fool reveals all that is in his mind* (Pr 17:28).

This good rule is taught: open sin open confession; private sin private confession. If there is open sin there should be open confession. If the sin is private then confess it to the Lord alone. It should remain just between you and God, otherwise, in our sincere desire to be open and honest we can cause unnecessary hurt to those we love!

Those who walk in the Spirit will walk in truth.

In our church family we should also follow this rule. Living in the truth but not hurting one another unnecessarily.

> *God is light; in him there is no darkness at all. If we claim to have fellowship with him yet walk in the darkness, we lie and do not live by the truth. But if we walk in the light, as he is in the light, we have fellowship with one another, and the blood of Jesus, his Son, purifies us from all sin* (1 Jn 1:5b-7).

C) THIRD PRINCIPLE: HEALING

If God hates hands that shed innocent blood then he loves hands that heal instead of hurting.

> *Therefore as God's chosen people, holy and dearly loved, clothe yourselves with compassion, kindness, humility, gentleness, and patience. Bear with each other and forgive whatever grievances you may have against one another. Forgive as the Lord forgave you. And over all these virtues put on love, which binds them together with perfect unity"* (Cl 3:12-14).

We may not murder in actuality, but we do sometimes cause grievous hurt by our words and our attitudes; by gossip and ungracious and hurtful speech.

Those we love most have the power to hurt us most deeply. People can be wounded by a spouse and these wounds take as long, or longer, than flesh wounds to heal. A broken leg can be seen and sympathised with. People are not so compassionate with someone who is suffering from inner wounds, which cannot be seen.

We must be so careful in our marriage, for love is precious, fragile, easily destroyed in a family. Imagine love as a crystal goblet, handle it carefully lest you shatter it and destroy it completely.

Instead let us have hands that seek to heal and bind up the unseen wounds caused by friction in the family; to pour in the oil of the Spirit. *"Don't let the sun go down on your anger"* Ep 4:26). Grudges can grow and are hard to make up; beware in case a root of bitterness springs up in your family life.

> *See to it that no one misses the grace of God and that no bitter root grows up to cause trouble and defile many* (He 12:15).

We who walk in the Spirit will always be eager to mend and build and we will never seek to break down and destroy.

This holds true also in our church family, Jesus was sent to bind up the wounds and to heal the broken hearted and we are to follow in his steps.

> *Jesus declared in the Nazareth synagogue, "The Spirit of the Lord is upon Me, Because he has anointed Me, To preach the gospel to the poor. He has sent Me to heal the broken hearted, To proclaim liberty to the captives, And recovery of sight to the blind, To set at liberty those who are oppressed, to proclaim the acceptable year of the Lord* (Lu 4:18-19 NKJV).

We are to be as he was when he walked this earth. What an awesome privilege; to take his yoke upon us and to fulfil the walk he has planned for us.

D) FOURTH PRINCIPLE: GODLINESS

If God hates a heart that devises wicked plans then he loves a heart that envisions godly scenarios.

That the hearts of mankind can devise wicked schemes is a real and terrible problem. Fantasising negative and sinful scenes has power, and giving in to temptation can destroy a life.

But if that is true then imagining good and wonderful things can be equally powerful and save lives.

God's will is for us, as for all those who would walk in the Spirit, to store up and meditate on the good and the beautiful. Spend some time writing down all the good things that have happened to you in your lifetime. Count your blessings!

> So amid the conflict, whether great or small,
> Do not be discouraged, God is over all,
> Count your many blessings, Angels will attend,
> Help and comfort give you to your journey's end.
>
> (Chorus) Count your blessings, name them one by one,
> Count your blessings, see what God has done;
> Count your blessings, name them one by one,

> And it will surprise you what the Lord has done.[33]

This old hymn should be sung more often, we tend to be an ungrateful generation, we should be praising and thanking God every moment for allowing us to be born into this land of plenty. Paul Sheehan reminds us of this fact –

> (You) are a member of the wealthiest community that has ever existed in this country (of Australia). Your household has a high likelihood of being wealthier than the Sun King (Louis 14th) or any of the other kings of France, or any monarch until the early 19th century, because although you may have far less property, you have much better health, vastly better hygiene, incomparably better transport and communications and even better food. You have greater individual freedom, greater privacy, your world is so much larger, safer and enlightened. You have a richer array of entertainments. You will live longer. And you are at no risk of having your head removed!
>
> Ordinary people in the cosmopolitan capitals of western society enjoy a standard of living that would be mind boggling to the average person of 200 years ago.[34]

So let us store up and meditate on the good and the beautiful. Imagine a happy and successful family; think of good things to do for one another. Envision a happy home where each member thinks of others before himself, where each seeks to inspire, to

---

33) Johnson Oatman Jnr.; *Count Your Blessings;* The Redemption Hymnal; Elim Pub. House 1961; 4th Stanza.

34) Sydney Morning Herald, Monday 27th Dec. 2004.

bring out the best in the others, and to help them reach their highest potential.

> Love is the passionate and abiding desire on the part of two or more people to produce together conditions under which each can be, and spontaneously express, his real self; to produce together an intellectual soil and an emotional climate in which each can flourish, far superior to what either could achieve alone. [35]

And in our church family let us see the best in one another, exhorting and encouraging each other even more as we see the day of the Lord approach for it is surely nearer than when we first believed, as Paul encouraged Timothy let us encourage one another –

> *Preach the Word; be prepared, in season, and out of season; correct, rebuke, and encourage – with great patience and careful instruction* (1 Ti 4:2).

E) FIFTH PRINCIPLE: GOODNESS

If God hates feet that are swift in running to evil (mischief, KJV) then he loves those who run to do good.

Mischief means harm, trouble, petty vexation, and a mischief maker is one who causes mischief, especially by inciting quarrels and bearing gossip. These people, like Satan, seek to divide and to destroy people's lives.

In contrast God loves a peacemaker. '*Blessed*', he says, '*are the peacemakers for they will be called sons of God*' (Mt 5:9).

Paul encourages us to speak only to build up and never to destroy, to bless and not to curse –

---

35) Jo Petty (compiled by); *Apples of Gold;* C.R. Gibson Co. Norwalk CT. USA; pg. 15.

> *Do not let any unwholesome talk come out of your mouths but only what is helpful for building others up according to their needs, that it may benefit those who listen (Ep 4:29).*

Happiness consists of doing good things for one another. In the home we should strive to build an atmosphere of peace and tranquillity, speaking well of one another and not dragging any member of our family down by speaking negatively about them.

In our church family gossip and mischief making can do great harm and we are warned against it in Scripture –

> *A malicious man disguises himself with his lips, but in his heart he harbours deceit. Though his speech is charming, do not believe him, for seven abominations fill his heart. His malice may be concealed by deception, but his wickedness will be exposed in the assembly (Pr 26:25-26).*

Rather, as we walk in the Spirit we should seek to bring harmony to the church by speaking only those things that will bless and build up.

> *But since we belong to the day, let us be self-controlled, putting on faith and love as a breastplate, and the hope of salvation as a helmet ... Live in peace with each other. And we urge you, brothers, warn those who are idle, encourage the timid, help the weak, be patient with everyone. Make sure that nobody pays back wrong for wrong, but always try to be kind to each other and to everyone else"* (1 Th 5:8-15).

F) SIXTH PRINCIPLE: TRUTHFULNESS

If God hates a false witness who speaks lies then he loves a true witness, one who speaks the truth, the truth of his Word.

Satan is a false witness who seeks to destroy our Christian life with his lying accusations

> *Be self controlled and alert. Your enemy the devil prowls around like a roaring lion, seeking who he may devour* (1 Pe 5:8-9).

In the book *Pilgrim's Progress* Christian comes to a place where there are lions in the path and he is afraid to continue. Mistrust and Timorous have already run away and he is left alone. He looks in his bosom for his scroll and discovers he has lost it. Many weary steps he retraces looking for his precious scroll. The story continues:

> [Christian finds his scroll where he lost it] Now, by this time he was come to the arbour again, where for a while he sat down and wept; but at last, as Christian would have it, looking sorrowfully down under the settle, there he espied his scroll; the which he, with trembling and haste, catched up, and put it into his bosom. But who can tell how joyful this man was when he had gotten his scroll again! For this scroll was the assurance of his life and acceptance at the desired haven. Therefore he laid it up in his bosom, gave thanks to God for directing his eye to the place where it lay, and with joy and tears betook himself again to his journey. But oh, how nimbly now did he go up the rest of the hill! Yet, before he got up, the sun went down upon Christian; and this made him again recall the vanity of his sleeping to his remembrance; and thus he again began to condole with himself: 'O thou sinful sleep; how, for thy sake, am I like to be benighted in my journey! I must walk without the sun; darkness must cover the path of my feet; and I must hear the noise of the doleful creatures, because of my sinful sleep'. [1 Thes. 5:6,7] Now also he remembered the story that Mistrust and Timorous told him of; how they were frightened

with the sight of the lions. Then said Christian to himself again, 'These beasts range in the night for their prey; and if they should meet with me in the dark, how should I shift them? How should I escape being by them torn in pieces?' Thus he went on his way. But while he was thus bewailing his unhappy miscarriage, he lifted up his eyes, and behold there was a very stately palace before him, the name of which was Beautiful; and it stood just by the highway side.

So I saw in my dream that he made haste and went forward, that if possible he might get lodging there. Now, before he had gone far, he entered into a very narrow passage, which was about a furlong off the porter's lodge; and looking very narrowly before him as he went, he espied two lions in the way. Now, thought he, I see the dangers that Mistrust and Timorous were driven back by. (The lions were chained, but he saw not the chains.) Then he was afraid, and thought also himself to go back after them, for he thought nothing but death was before him. But the porter at the lodge, whose name is Watchful, perceiving that Christian made a halt as if he would go back, cried unto him, saying, 'Is thy strength so small? [Mark 8:34-37] Fear not the lions, for they are chained, and are placed there for trial of faith where it is, and for discovery of those that had none. Keep in the midst of the path, no hurt shall come unto thee.'

> Difficulty is behind, Fear is before,
> Though he's got on the hill, the lions roar;
> A Christian man is never long at ease,
> When one fright's gone, another doth him seize"

> Then I saw that he went on, trembling for fear of the lions, but taking good heed to the directions of the porter; he heard them roar, but they did him no harm. Then he clapped his hands, and went on till he came and stood before the gate where the porter was. Then said Christian to the porter, 'Sir, what house is this? And may I lodge here to-night?' The porter answered, 'This house was built by the Lord of the hill, and he built it for the relief and security of pilgrims.' The porter also asked whence he was, and whither he was going.
>
> Christian: 'I am come from the City of Destruction, and am going to Mount Zion; but because the sun is now set, I desire, if I may, to lodge here to-night'.[36]

As Christian discovered, the devil is only <u>like</u> a roaring lion, a chained lion; but we have on our side the <u>real</u> lion, the Lion of the Tribe of Judah, our glorious Saviour, who watches over us to protect us and bring us safely to his Heavenly Kingdom. Still further on the matter of truthfulness note that–

> *A truthful witness gives an honest testimony, but a false witness tells lies* (Pr 12:17).

It is the devil who tries to turn us away and lead us into deep depression as he recounts our past mistakes and sins. Let us say the things God says and not what Satan says. God is truth and we should say the things he says about us in his Word.

Dwell on the positive. If you dwell on the good then that increases, if you dwell on the bad then that grows stronger. Nobody is perfect, we can only cast ourselves at the feet of Jesus and claim

---

36) John Bunyan; *The Pilgrim's Progress.*

his righteousness for our own. We should inspire one another to reach for the highest and the best.

As we walk in the Spirit, encouraging each other in God's Word of truth, we will grow to be more like Jesus and this equals happiness in family life.

In our church family we should not give ground to Satan's lies, rather we should accentuate the positive, repeating God's words about one another.

> *A word aptly spoken is like apples of gold in settings of silver* (Pr 25:11).

> *Let the peace of Christ rule in your hearts, since as members of one body you were called to peace. And be thankful. Let the word of Christ dwell in you richly as you teach and admonish one another with all wisdom and as you sing psalms, hymns and spiritual songs with gratitude in your hearts to God. And whatever you do, whether in word or deed, do it all in the name of the Lord Jesus, giving thanks to God the Father through him* (Cl 3:15-17).

G) SEVENTH PRINCIPLE: HARMONY

If God hates those who sow discord among brethren then he loves those who sow harmony; those who love the Lord and his church.

Paul says,

> *Warn a divisive person once, and then warn him a second time. After that have nothing to do with him* (Titus 3:10).

Dissension, divisiveness, disharmony are all the work of Satan.

In marriage the basic cause is selfishness, selfishness is at the foundation of all evil and disharmony. When all go their own way, pulling in different directions, thinking only of themselves, then sadness will reign.

One result of this kind of selfishness is adultery. This is a terrible sin, hurtful, hateful, robbing one's partner, sinning against one's own body, which is the Temple of the Holy Spirit (2Co 6:16).

There is no excuse!

> It is absurd to pretend that one cannot love the same woman always as to pretend that a good artist needs several violins to play a piece of music.
>
> A long life is barely enough for a man and a woman to understand each other; and to be understood is to love. The man who understands one woman is qualified to understand pretty well everything. [37]

God loves rather those who sow harmony in the home and family.

> *How good and how pleasant it is when bothers (and sisters) live together in unity ... there the Lord bestows his blessing* (Ps 133).

In marriage and family life we should harmonise together as an orchestra harmonises music and blends it together into a beautiful melody. So we should seek to make our marriage and family beautiful for God.

And in our church family we should always seek to bring people together, not divide them, and seek to harmonise church relationships by living as Jesus would live in our situation.

> *I urge you to live a life worthy of the calling you have received. Be completely humble and gentle, be patient, bearing with one another in love,*

---

37) *Apples of Gold*; op.cit. pgs. 13&14.

> *Make every effort to keep the unity of the Spirit through the bond of peace* Ep 4:1-3).

As we walk in the Spirit in our family life and in the life of the church let us avoid the things God hates; seek to embrace the things he loves; build beautiful marriages and families and a strong church body – one that will withstand the onslaughts and attacks of the enemy.

CHAPTER ELEVEN

WALKING IN THE WORK PLACE

Walking in the Spirit and producing the fruit of the Spirit can strengthen the work place whether one is the owner, the manager or the worker, and it can increase productivity as God's blessing will rest upon everything one does.

A) LOVE

Loving God with heart and mind and soul and strength, and loving one's neighbour as oneself is good for business. It will encourage managers and workers to think from the customer's point of view. Depending on what the product is, they will ensure it is one they can sell with confidence, knowing it to be durable, whether it be something beautiful or something practical.

1) Agape love: is the kind of love that wants the best for the other person; wants them to prosper and do well. To show this kind of concern the manager should watch over his workers, especially those who are young and apprenticed to him and teach them the values of honesty and integrity.

This kind of love is not sweet, sickly and sentimental. That parody of care is brought forward to excuse criminal conduct in our present court system. No, this is a strong love, a tough love, which will not stand back and watch a young person go in the wrong direction without holding them accountable. A weak, sentimental love will help them on the downward way to a ruined life; the other, godly type of love, will serve to put them on the right track and so lead them toward a stronger character.

B) JOY

A pleasant joyful attitude toward other staff members and toward the customer makes life pleasant and increases sales. God has granted us the joy of knowing him and promises us his protection as we take refuge in him through Christ our Saviour.

> *But let all who take refuge in you be glad; let them ever sing for joy, Spread your protection over them, that those who love your name may rejoice in you* (Ps 5:11).

> *Blessed are those who have learned to acclaim you, who walk in the light of your presence O Lord. They rejoice in your name all day long; they exult in your righteousness* (Ps 89:15-16).

There is a difference between joy and happiness:

Happiness depends on what is happening in our life, it hinges on our present circumstances. Joy does not depend on outward circumstances; joy depends on our belief system. The best way to gain happiness is not to try to manufacture it for ourselves, but instead to serve others and seek to bring them a little happiness. When we practise this life style happiness creeps on us unawares.

The boss who seeks to keep his staff happy in their work and their surroundings will gain increased productivity.

> *Happiness makes the heart cheerful* (Pr 15:13a).

C) PEACE

Peace comes from the Lord, who promised it to us and it produces <u>orderliness and calm</u>, both within the person and in his environment. We are enjoined to be anxious for nothing but to let the Lord's peace guard our hearts.

> *Peace I leave with you; my peace I give you* (Jn 14:27a).

> *Do not be anxious about anything, but in everything, by prayer and petition, with thanksgiving, present your requests to God. And the peace of God, which transcends all understanding, will guard your hearts and your minds in Christ Jesus* (Ph 4:6-7).

1) Orderliness is a characteristic that produces form and neatness instead of an untidy mess. In a church it brings order to the service, in a business it brings order also, and a person with this trait will have his stock regulated. He will know what he has in store so that for example all orders can be filled promptly.

> *For God is not a God of disorder, but of peace* (1 Co 14:33a)

2) Calmness, with good communication between management and staff leads to a well-ordered, peaceful and calm work place, where the minimum of disruption means business will grow and develop. If we let the peace of God rule over our heart then we will be less likely to give way to anger in the workplace,

> *Let the peace of Christ rule in your hearts, since as one body you were called to peace* (Cl 3:15).

D) PATIENCE

Having patience toward the most irritating customer must be a good advertisement to those standing by, leading to good relationships and to customer satisfaction, which could translate into more sales/orders. God grants wisdom to those who ask for it and this will help us to have patience toward those who may be offensive in their attitude.

> *A man's wisdom gives him patience; it is his glory to overlook an offense* (Pr 19:11).

> *A man of knowledge uses words with restraint, and a man of understanding is even-tempered* (Pr 17:27).

E) KINDNESS

A manager, must be kind but firm. Firmness is essential, for if he is merely kind and lets the worker come and go as he pleases, and work when he feels like it, this will lead to continual lateness, and bad workmanship. He must be kind and merciful but just in all his dealings with the staff, not allowing the worker to encroach on his good will.

> *He has showed you, O man, what is good. And what does the Lord require of you? To act justly and to love mercy and to walk humbly with thy God* (Mi 6:8).

F) GOODNESS

Morally upright managers will not do anything against the law; they will take care of their staff and they will also make right decisions when faced with the temptation to make money illegally. They will not tolerate cheating or bad workmanship, neither will they allow other businesses to cheat them. They will pay their workers a fair wage and they will pay within a reasonable time those from whom they receive goods.

The worker, too, will be honest in all his dealings and he will pay his own bills on time. This kind of goodness includes <u>honesty integrity and business ethics:</u>

    1) Honesty: those who walk in the Spirit will be honest in all their dealings with others.

> *Do not use dishonest standards when measuring length, weight or quantity. Use honest scales and honest weights* (Le 19:35-36a).

    2) Integrity: those who walk in the Spirit will be honest even when no one is around to observe them because their honesty comes from within their own spirit.

> *Slaves (workers) obey your earthly masters (bosses) in everything,; and do it, not only when*

their eye is on you and to win their favour, but with sincerity of heart and reverence for the Lord. Whatever you do, work at it with all your heart, as working for the Lord, not for men, since you know you will receive an inheritance from the Lord as a reward (Cl 3:22-24a).

Make it your ambition to lead a quiet life, to mind your own business and to work with your hands, just as we told you, so that your daily life may win the respect of outsiders and so you will not be dependent on anybody (1 Th 4:11-12).

3) Ethics: they will observe all ethical behaviour appropriate to their position, both manager and worker. There will be no using office equipment for outside jobs without permission, no taking home materials belonging to the firm. No stealing, because this is what these practices amount to, and no discounts given without permission.

Whoever can be trusted with very little can also be trusted with much, and whoever is dishonest with very little will also be dishonest with much. So if you have not been trustworthy in handling worldly wealth, who will trust you with true riches? And if you have not been trustworthy with someone else's property, who will give you property of your own (Lu 16:10-12).

He who has been stealing must steal no longer, but must work, doing something useful with his own hands, that he may have something to share with those in need (Ep 4:28).

Many years ago an immigrant from South America, a Christian man, started a business working on cars in his capacity as a mechanic. He belonged to a large church and many of the congregation began to come to him for repairs on their car. To his dismay many of these people did not pay their bills. He sent out reminders but with no result. Finally he saw that if something was not done then he would go bankrupt and he pleaded with his pastor to ask the congregation to be honest and pay their bills. The pastor refused to do this and this good Christian man unhappily had to close down his business through lack of funds. Understandably he felt bitter and disillusioned.

This is only one of several stories which could be told of dishonesty among Christian people. Just recently, during a large conference a door prize was won by a ticket holder. When she went to collect her prize, to her astonishment, no less than eight people had attempted to collect the parcel. If the office staff had not waited until the right person came along with the correct ticket and the right identification she would have lost her prize. These eight were people who had just attended a <u>Christian</u> Conference! This kind of thing is tantamount to stealing. We should ask ourselves what Jesus would do, what he would say, if he were here in the flesh, attending our church! I'm sure he would be as scathing concerning Christian dishonesty as he was toward the Scribes and the Pharisees in Bible days.

On the other hand there are many Christians who pay their bills promptly and who give sacrificially, and who truly show the fruit of the Spirit in their goodness and faithfulness. They will never be the cause of someone turning away from the gospel because of dishonest people in the body of Christ.

Zacchaeus was a Bible character who, through his fellowship with Jesus, turned from his greed for amassing money to magnificent generosity toward his fellow Jews. Reading this story we can see that Zacchaeus became an honourable man, determined not to have even the slightest hint of dishonesty staining his character now that he could call Jesus friend. But note in Luke's account that he said, **'If I have cheated anybody,'** indicating that he was fairly sure he had not cheated anyone –

> Zacchaeus said, *'Look Lord! Here and now I give half of my possessions to the poor, and if I have*

cheated anybody out of anything, I will pay back four times the amount' (Lu 19:8).

G) FAITHFULNESS:

This is something precious to the Lord and he has promised the faithful his blessing and favour. The faithful man is also a <u>diligent man</u> who will do his work without needing to be driven. He will be faithful in all the aspects of his life.

The Lord preserves the faithful, but the proud he pays back in full (Ps 32:23).

A faithful man will be richly blessed but one eager to get rich will not go unpunished (Pr 28:20).

Let love and faithfulness never leave you; bind them around your neck, write them on the tablet of your heart. Then you will win favour and a good name in the sight of God and man (Pr 3:3-4).

1) Faithfulness toward God: continuing on in the Christian faith without wavering.

Let us hold unswervingly to the hope we profess, for he who promised is faithful (He 10:23).

2) Toward family: faithful to the marriage vow and to the parenting of any children.

Husbands, love your wives, just as Christ loved the church ... In this same way, husbands ought to love their wives as their own bodies. He who loves his wife loves himself ... Fathers, do not exasperate your children; instead, bring them up in the training and instruction of the Lord (Ep 5:25-28; 6:4).

3) Toward church: regular in church attendance and if anything is promised, keeping that promise; whether it is a promise to complete a task or a promise to give money or gifts to the church.

> *Let us not give up meeting together, as some are in the habit of doing, but let us encourage one another – and all the more as you see the day approaching* (He 10:2).

4) Toward business: the manager should be faithful in business and staff responsibilities.

5) The worker: must be faithful to give a good day's work for a full day's wage. He should think of his tasks as dedicated to the Lord first and done well for his sake, while at the same time he works well for his boss.

> *And whatever you do, whether in word or deed, do it all in the name of the Lord Jesus, giving thanks to God the Father through him* (Cl 3:17).

6) Diligence: the faithful and diligent man will be rewarded by the Lord.

> *The sluggard craves and gets nothing, but the desires of the diligent are fully satisfied* (Pr 13:4).

> *Do you see a man skilled in his work? He will serve before kings; he will not serve before obscure men* (Pr 22:29; see also Lu 19:12-26).

H) GENTLENESS:

Meek does not mean weak. Gentle people are strong people not doormats for anyone to tread on. So a gentle person will give a soft answer to turn away wrath; however, he will not give in to bullying nor to stand-over tactics. He will stand for what he believes is right and will protect those weaker than himself.

Gentleness involves being a gentleman/gentlewoman for God. He/she will dress appropriately, there will be no swearing, no intimidation, no sexual harassment, no unnecessary anger, no carrying of grudges in the work place. Instead, they will speak purposefully, sharing calm, upright conversation, which in turn may encourage others to seek the Lord for themselves.

> *Let your gentleness be evident to all. The Lord is near* (Ph 4:6).

I) SELF-CONTROL:

There are many Scriptures which inspire us to be self controlled in our lives, such as –.

> *Since we belong to the day, let us be self controlled, putting on faith and love as a breastplate, and the hope of salvation as a helmet* (1 Th 5:8).

Paul, along with his instructions for the leaders of the church, also encouraged Titus to speak to the young men and urge them also to be self controlled. In keeping themselves strictly they will be an example to others.

It follows that as they earn the right to witness to their workmates, through friendly care and concern for them, their workmates will be more likely to listen to what they have to say.

> *Encourage the young men to be self controlled. In everything set them an example by doing what is good. In your teaching show integrity, seriousness, and soundness of speech that cannot be condemned, so that those who oppose you may be ashamed because they have nothing bad to say about us* (Tit 2:6-8).

1) Self-control in body: in personal life the fruit bearer will not live to excess and therefore become sick and unable to work; instead he will be full of energy and able to build a strong and successful business. The worker will also have less sick days, which will again save the company money from lost productivity.

2) Self-control at work: the self-controlled person will not work excessively but will order his life with right priorities. In this way he will find the time for recreation and to spend with his family. Yet neither will he be lazy.

> *I went past the field of the sluggard. Past the vineyard of the man who lacks judgment.:. A little sleep, a little slumber, a little folding of the hands to rest – and poverty will come on you like a bandit and scarcity like an armed man* (Pr 24:30-34).

3) Self control in money matters: the owner, the manager, or the worker all need to put God first, before business. If they must borrow they will project their future carefully, not borrowing more money for expansion than they can pay back easily.

> *No one can serve two masters. Either he will hate the one and love the other, or he will be devoted to the one and despise the other. You cannot serve God and money"* (Mt 6:24).

> *Suppose one of you wants to build a tower. Will he not first sit down and estimate the cost to see if he has enough money to complete it? For if he lays the foundation and is not able to finish it, everyone who sees it will ridicule him, saying, "This fellow began to build and was not able to finish"* (Lu 14:28-30).

So we see that the men and women who walk in the Spirit, displaying the fruit of the Spirit, will be good managers, or good workers, depending on their position, and will bring praise and glory to the Lord in all their endeavours.

CHAPTER TWELVE

THE NEW MAN

The Bible gives us a beautiful picture of the loveliness of a perfect Christian life. This picture shows the gracious character and ideal pattern that every Christian is called to emulate.[38] The Scriptures portray this perfect (in the words of the NKJV) character in various ways, but one of the most fascinating is the contrasting analogy drawn between our **'old man'** and our **'new man.'**

The **'old man'** is our previously un-renewed, corrupted, and sin darkened nature.

The **'new man'** is the new creation we have become in the Lord Jesus Christ –

> *Therefore if anyone is in Christ, he is a <u>new creation</u>; old things have passed away; behold all things have become new* (2 Co 5:17 NKJV).

> *But now you yourselves are to put off ... the old man with his deeds ... put on the <u>new man</u>, who is renewed in knowledge according to the image of him who created him* (Cl 3:9-10 NKJV).

---

38) This chapter and the two following are from studies completed in 1960 by Dr. Ken Chant.

> *Put on the <u>new man</u>, which was created according to God, in true righteousness and holiness (Ep 4:24 NKJV).*

We are told to **put off** the 'old man' and to put on the 'new man.'

This new self brings us **knowledge**, shapes us into the **image of God**; produces **righteousness** and true **holiness** within us; gives us **victory** over all old things; and makes us new in every way.

If we fail to realise in our daily walk all of those characteristics of the new self, it is because of one or both of the following reasons –

We have not attempted true obedience to the command to **'put off the old man and put on the new man'**; that is, we have been indifferent to God's challenge to live a life centred in Christ; or we have attempted to obey this command in ways differing from God's revealed method.

It is too little realised that when God gives a warning or a promise he **always** tells me how to avoid the one and appropriate the other.

For example:

– when Noah was warned of the flood, he was also given complete instructions on how to build the ark.

– when Sodom was about to be destroyed, Lot was told exactly how to escape.

– when it came time to deliver the Israelites from Egypt, Moses was given precise directions how to set the people free.

There is a Bible way to receive forgiveness of sins – call on the name of the Lord Jesus Christ.

There is a Bible way to find physical healing – by the laying on of hands and the prayer of faith.

There is a Bible way to experience remission of sins, and the burying of the **'old man'** - by baptism.

So there is a Bible way to put on the 'new man'.

Which brings us to two questions:

- what is this 'new man'?

- how can we **put on** the 'new man'?

A) THE 'NEW MAN' IN THE OLD TESTAMENT.

Ez 36:25-30. The **'new man'** is described as being cleansed from all sin and idolatry, as having a new heart, as keeping the law of God, and as being abundantly fruitful and prosperous.

Ps 103:1-5. Once again the **'new man'** is shown to be cleansed from sin, healed of sickness, crowned with rich blessing, contented in heart and mind, and renewed in youth, strength and vigour.

Such will be the blessing of God upon the **'new man'** that in his weakness he will be as David of old, and in his strength he will be as the angel of the Lord (Zc 12:8).

B) THE 'NEW MAN' IN THE NEW TESTAMENT.

1) Righteous with God and made into his image.

And we, who with unveiled faces all reflect the Lord's glory, are being transformed into his likeness with ever-increasing glory, which comes from the Lord, who is the Spirit (2 Co 3:18).

You were taught, with regard to your former way of life, to put off your old self, which is being corrupted by its deceitful desires; to be made new in the attitude of your minds; and to put on the new self, created to be like God in true righteousness and holiness (Ep 4:22-24).

For in Christ all the fullness of the Deity lives in bodily form, and you have been given fullness in Christ, who is the head over every power and authority ... and have put on the <u>new self</u>, which is being renewed in knowledge in the image of its Creator (Cl 2:9-10; 3:10).

2) Indwelt by Christ

To them God has chosen to make known among the Gentiles the glorious riches of this mystery, which is <u>Christ in you,</u> the hope of glory (Cl 1:27).

I have been crucified with Christ and I no longer live, but Christ lives in me. The life I live in the body, I live by faith in the Son of God, who loved me and gave himself for me (Ga 2:20).

Though you have not seen him, you love him; and even though you do not see him now, you believe in him and are filled with an inexpressible and glorious joy (1Pe 1:8).

Those who obey his commands live in him, and he in them. And this is how we know that he lives in us: we know it by the Spirit he gave us (1 Jn 3:24).

3) At peace in the will of God.

Therefore since we have been justified through faith, we have peace with God through our Lord Jesus Christ, through whom we have gained access by faith into this grace in which we now stand. And we rejoice in the hope of the glory of God. Not only so, but we also rejoice in our sufferings (Ro 5:1-3a).

And we know that in all things God works for the good of those who love him, who have been called according to his purpose ... For I am convinced that neither death nor life, neither angels nor demons, neither the present nor the future, nor any powers, neither height nor depth, nor anything else in all creation, will be able to separate us from the love of God that is in Christ Jesus our Lord (Ro 8:28, 38-39).

I know what it is to be in need, and I know what it is to have plenty. I have learned the secret of being content in any and every situation, whether well fed or hungry, whether living in plenty or in want. I can do everything through him who gives me strength (Ph 4:12-13).

4) A mighty warrior

<u>I have given you authority</u> to trample on snakes and scorpions and to overcome all the power of the enemy; <u>nothing</u> will harm you (Lu 10:19).

But <u>you will receive power</u> when the Holy Spirit comes on you; and you will be my witnesses in Jerusalem, and in all Judea and Samaria, and to the ends of the earth (Ac 1:8).

Yet to all who received him, to those who believed in his name, <u>he gave the right</u> to become children of God (Jn 1:12).

<u>Finally be strong in the Lord and in his mighty power</u>. Put on the full armour of God so that you can take your stand against the devil's schemes (Ep 6:10-11).

C) HOW TO PUT ON THE 'NEW MAN'

1) The influence of the Spirit

Whenever the leading characteristics of the 'new man' are mentioned, they are specifically ascribed to the Holy Spirit. They result from the influence of the indwelling Spirit upon the believer–

> *Now the Lord is the Spirit, and where the Spirit of the Lord is there is liberty ... (we) are being transformed into his likeness with ever increasing glory, <u>which comes from the Lord, who is the Spirit</u>* (2 Co 3:17-18b).
>
> *... We rejoice in our sufferings ... because God has poured out his love into our hearts by the Holy Spirit* (Ro 5:3-5).
>
> *There is therefore now no condemnation to those who are in Christ Jesus <u>who do not walk according to the flesh but according to the Spirit.</u> For the law of the Spirit of life in Christ Jesus has made me free from the law of sin and death ... <u>If by the Spirit you put to death the deeds of the body, you will live</u> ... you received the Spirit of adoption by whom we cry out, 'Abba, Father' ... <u>the Spirit</u> also <u>helps our weaknesses</u> ... (and) makes intercession for the saints* (Ro 8:1-26 NKJV).
>
> *Overflow with hope <u>by the power of the Holy Spirit</u> ... by the power of signs and miracles, through the power of the Spirit* (Ro 15:13b,19a).
>
> *But <u>the fruit of the Spirit</u> is love, joy, peace, patience, kindness, goodness, faithfulness, gentleness, and self-control* (Ga 5:22-23a).

> *I pray ... he may strengthen you with power <u>through his Spirit</u> in your inner being ... that you, being rooted and established in love ... may be filled to the measure of all the fullness of God* (Ep 3:16-19).
>
> *Take ... the <u>sword of the Spirit</u> which is the Word of God ... and pray <u>in the Spirit</u> on all occasions with all kinds of prayers and requests* (Ro 6:17-18).
>
> *<u>I will put my Spirit in you</u> and move you to follow my decrees, and be careful to keep my laws* (Ez 36:27).

And many other references could be quoted.

2) Through Holy Spirit Baptism

The Holy Spirit begins to achieve many of these things in the life of the believer from the moment of the new birth. But there is no doubt that the special baptism of the Holy Spirit greatly accelerates the influence of the Spirit upon Christian life. This gives the believer a renewed and vital opportunity to fulfil the Bible pattern for the 'new man' that God has made us in the Lord Jesus Christ.

All of the following Scriptures speak clearly of the baptism of the Spirit, and speak also of several characteristics of the 'new man' which spring directly from that baptism ...

> *Whoever believes in me, as the Scripture has said, <u>streams of living water</u> will flow from within him. By this he meant the Spirit, whom those who believed in him were later to receive* (Jn 7:38-39).
>
> *But the Counselor, the Holy Spirit, whom the Father will send in my name, will teach you all things* (Jn 14:26; 15:26; 16:7-14).

> *Do not leave Jerusalem, but wait for the gift my Father promised, which you have heard me speak about ... <u>you will receive power</u> when the Holy Spirit comes on you* (Ac 1:4-8).
>
> "<u>God has poured out his love into our hearts</u> by the Holy Spirit" (Ro 5:5).

All of the above Scriptures, and many more that could be quoted, refer distinctly to baptism in the Holy Spirit, and the works of grace referred to cannot be fully achieved in the believer's life apart from that baptism.

To realise completely in our experience God's revealed pattern for the 'new man', we must be endued with power from on high by the mighty infilling of the Holy Spirit.

3) Walking in faith

However it is vital to recognise this fact: **Holy Spirit baptism will not automatically clothe us with the 'new man'.**

The command to **'put on the new man'** was given to men and women who were **already** filled with the Holy Spirit; for example, the Ephesians.

Ac 19:6 and Ep 1:13 show that the Ephesians had definitely experienced a supernatural baptism in the Holy Spirit. Yet the command is strongly given that they should now, in the strength of the Spirit of God, **'put off the old man and put on the new man'** (Ep 4:22-24). The apostle urged them to continue being **'filled with the Spirit'**, for they would then find praise in God, they would have a song in their hearts, they would be united with each other, and they would walk in the fear of God, knowing the riches of his blessing (Ep 5:17-21).

So we are told again, **'If we live in the Spirit'** (that is are 'made alive' by the Spirit and have been baptised in the Spirit, our bodies becoming the living temples of the Holy Spirit), **'let us also walk in the Spirit'** (Ga 5:25 NKJV).

And again: ***'Walk in the Spirit and you shall not fulfil the lust of the flesh'*** (Ga 5:16 NKJV).

Thus three things are essential for every person.

    a) to be born of the Spirit, and thus receive eternal life;

    b) then to be baptised in the Spirit, and thus receive all the potential of the new life in Christ;

    c) then to walk in the Spirit, and thus release all of that divine potential into effective daily living.

Let us examine this more closely –

> *For the sinful nature desires what is contrary to the Spirit, and the Spirit what is contrary to the sinful nature* (Ga 5:17).

In every Christian there is a struggle between the flesh and the Spirit. The grace of God within us prevents us from evil; but also the evil within us many times prevents the grace of God. It is a struggle between the remains of sin and the beginnings of grace. The **flesh,** characterised by the 'old man', and the **Spirit**, characterised by the 'new man', are always contrary to each other. This conflict will endure without abatement until Christ comes and our **'mortal has put on immortality'**, our **'corruptibility becomes incorruption'**, and our **'lowly bodies are conformed to his glorious body'** (1 Co 15:53-54; Ph 3:21 NKJV).

But there is an appeasing factor; we may so walk before the Lord that whereas the flesh was one time utterly victorious, the Spirit will now steadily assume the ascendancy in our lives. Thus we become **'more than conquerors in Christ'** (Ro 8:37 NKJV).

Exactly what is meant by the 'flesh' in a man's life, and also the 'Spirit'? The influence of the flesh and the influence of the Spirit are shown by the things they produce. We will examine this aspect in more detail in the next chapter.

CHAPTER THIRTEEN

THE 'FLESH' AND THE 'SPIRIT'

A) THE FLESH

The acts of the sinful nature are obvious: sexual immorality, impurity and debauchery; idolatry and witchcraft; hatred, discord, jealousy, fits of rage, selfish ambition, dissensions, factions and envy; drunkenness, orgies and the like. I warn you, as I did before, <u>that those who live like this will not inherit the kingdom of God</u> (Ga 5:19-21).

But notice: it is those who **live like this**, not those who **have lived**. All of us are guilty of having done some or all of those fleshly things. But if we have turned from them, and have trusted in the blood of Christ, then they are remembered no more, and we need have no fear of them, nor any sense of condemnation.

But what if we are still bound by some of these works of the flesh? What shall we then do? How do we then stand before God? These questions are answered by Paul's explanation of the fruit of the Spirit ...

B) THE SPIRIT

But the fruit of the Spirit is love, joy, peace, patience, kindness, goodness, faithfulness, gentleness and self-control (Ga 5:22-23).

<u>The first three</u> – **love, joy, peace** – are directed toward **God**, and display our relationship with him.

The second three –**patience, kindness, goodness** – are directed toward our **neighbours**, and display our relationship with them.

The third three – **faithfulness, gentleness and self-control** – are directed toward **ourselves**, and display our relationship within ourselves.

1) Fruit that God may pluck.

a) Love

What kind of love are we to have for God?

There are four words for love in Greek:

– there is the love of a man for a maid.

– there is the love of a parent for his child.

– there is the love of a person for something very dear.

– there is this love for God, which is expressed by the word **agape**.

Agape describes a love that embraces every part of a man's being, his will, his emotions, his intelligence, his strength. So Jesus said –

Love the Lord your God with all heart and with all your soul and with all your mind" (Mt 22:37).

We are to love God as those who are espoused to him, **'a holy, chaste and spotless bride'** (1 Th 5:23-24).

We are to love God as his **'own dear children'** (1 Jn 3:1-2).

We are to love God who **'grants to us the treasure of his glory in Jesus Christ'** (2 Co 4:6-7).

To love God is to find his deliverance, and so to be filled with **joy** (Ps 18:1-3).

To love God is to find his inward rest, and so to be filled with **peace** (De 33:27-29).

b) Joy

This lovely and animate emotion is marvellously characteristic of God. It is true that Jesus was known as the 'Man of Sorrows', but even here the eternal joy of the Deity upheld him, **'for the joy that was set before him he endured the cross and despised the shame'** (He 12:2).

It brings no pleasure to God to see his people mournful. To be God-like is not to be sad-faced but rather to *'rejoice with joy inexpressible and full of glory!'* (1 Pe 1:8 NKJV). The Scripture says that

> *The ransomed of the Lord will return; they will enter Zion with singing; everlasting joy will crown their heads. Gladness and joy will overtake them, and sorrow and sighing will flee away* (Is 35:10).

c) Peace

This peace is not merely freedom from trouble; rather, it embraces all those things that make up a person's highest good. This peace is a calm tranquillity that comes from knowing that every day is fully in the control of God, that our times are in his hand –

> *Many are asking, "Who can show us any good?" Let the light of your face shine upon us, O Lord. You have filled my heart with greater joy than when their grain and new wine abound. I will lie down and sleep in peace, for you alone, O Lord, make me dwell in safety* (Ps 4:6-8).

To walk in the Spirit will create in you this peace, possessing and prospering your whole life.

2) Fruit that your neighbour may pluck

a) Patience –Longsuffering (KJV)

This is the grace of a man who could revenge himself, but who does not do so; it is a man who is slow to anger, and easy to be entreated.

The best illustration of what is meant by this word and how we should show it toward our neighbour, is to observe it in the dealings of God with us –

> *Or do you show contempt for the riches of his kindness, tolerance and patience, not realising that God's kindness leads you toward repentance* (Ro 2:4).

As the forbearance of God served to lead us to repentance, so should we give our **neighbour** a similar opportunity and kindness. So the Scripture expressly states that the long-suffering of God is a pattern for us to follow –

> *But for that very reason I was shown mercy so that in me, the worst of sinners, Christ Jesus might display his unlimited patience as an example for those who would believe on him and receive eternal life* (1Ti 1:16).

b) Kindness – Gentleness (KJV)

Jesus said, **'*My yoke is easy, and my burden is light*'** (Mt 11:30). He used the same Greek word as Paul. A 'gentle' yoke is one that will not chafe, or irk, or gall, or irritate. Neither should we by word or deed put any other than a 'gentle' yoke on our neighbour. This fruit of gentleness will create in us a genuine desire to help people who are facing difficulty, to show mercy to those who have fallen, and to be kind to those who are in need.

c) Goodness

The Greek word translated 'goodness' is a peculiarly Bible word; it does not occur in any other ancient Greek text. It means 'goodness that is associated with knowledge.' It is that goodness which admonishes those who are at fault, goodness that is linked with holy zeal and righteousness, and with the truth of God's Word. It is the goodness Jesus showed when he chased the money-changers out of the temple, or when he denounced the Pharisees.

Gentleness can only help and show kindness; but **goodness** can correct, reprove, and discipline.

Longsuffering is refraining from anger; **gentleness** is showing positive kindness, even to an enemy; but goodness embraces both longsuffering **and** gentleness, and in great strength seeks to raise a man up, to guide him, and to set him on the right way.

Usually goodness must first be preceded by gentleness, and gentleness by longsuffering.

For a balanced and truly effective Christian character, all three attributes are needed.

To have this three-fold fruit exemplified in his or her life will enable the Spirit-filled Christian to serve both God and neighbour well.

3) Fruit that you may pluck

a) Faithfulness – Faith (KJV)

The word is best translated as **faithfulness, fidelity,** or **good faith**. It describes a person whose integrity is beyond question, who would never dream of violating trust, whose word is totally reliable; a person who can never be reproached for falsehood, who can never be accused of dishonesty, who is never guilty of pretending to be what he is not. In a world filled with deceit, the unsullied truthfulness of the Spirit-filled Christian shines like the bright light of God.

b) Gentleness – Meekness (KJV)

This word conveys three ideas –

i) Submissive

Blessed are the meek for they will inherit the earth ... Take my yoke upon you and learn from me, for I am gentle and humble in heart, and you will find rest for your souls (Mt 5:5; 11:29).

ii) Teachable

My dear brothers, take note of this: Everyone should be quick to listen, slow to speak and slow to become angry, for man's anger does not bring about the righteous life that God desires. Therefore get rid of all moral filth and the evil that is so prevalent and humbly accept the word planted in you, which can save you. Do not merely listen to the word, and so deceive yourselves. Do what it says ... (Ja 1:19-22).

iii) Considerate

Brothers, if someone is caught in a sin, you who are spiritual should restore him gently. But watch yourself, or you also may be tempted ... Be completely humble and gentle; be patient, bearing with one another in love (Ga 6:1; Ep 4:2).

Meekness is not being so mild and inoffensive that one becomes ludicrous; it is meekness as Jesus exemplified it; that is, having sympathetic regard for the circumstances and feelings of other people. It is the halfway mark between being excessively angry or excessively mild; it is in knowing when to be angry and when to be gentle.

c) Self-control – Temperance (KJV)

This word conveys the idea of:

– **habitual** moderation in handling the natural appetites and passions.

– **quiet** patience; being ready to wait for the seed of good to come to full fruition in the lives of those we love, and for whom we pray.

– **calmness**; having our temper in check at all times; not allowing irritation or frustration to govern us.

The person who wants power over devils, power with men, and power with God, must first learn to rule himself. The man who fails to rule himself can never successfully rule another. But greater still, this virtue of self-control is the capacity which fits a man, not to rule, but to serve.

Paul has a good comment on the meaning of **'self-control'** in 1 Co 9:24-27.

4) All the fruit together

This, then, is the 'fruit of the spirit' – love, joy, peace, patience, kindness, goodness, faithfulness, gentleness, self-control.

It is the fruit (singular) of the Spirit – which indicates that these traits cannot be produced by praying for them one by one; they spring forth in a single cluster as a Christian walks in the Spirit.

> *But blessed is the man who trusts in the Lord, whose confidence is in him. He will be like a tree planted by the water that sends out its roots by the stream. It does not fear when heat comes; its leaves are always green, It has no worries in a year of drought and never fails to bear fruit* (Je 17:7-8).

CHAPTER FOURTEEN

WALKING IN THE SPIRIT

We have seen that there is a conflict in the life of every Christian, a struggle between the flesh and the Spirit. We have seen the works of the flesh, and also the fruit of the Spirit.

Every person who endeavours to live a godly life will be conscious of this conflict. To experience it should not cause you to be afraid or fall into condemnation. It is an inevitable part of the process of growing to maturity and perfection in Christ (Ga 5:17).

Even though you may at times fail to do the things that you should, so long as you would do them if you could, and so long as you are striving to be led of the Spirit and to walk worthy of the Lord, 'you are not under law,' nor will you be condemned by God for your failures (vs 18).

But that does not mean that any of us may dare to be complacent about sin or failure; for if we are being led by the Spirit it is clearly expected that the victory of Christ will become increasingly evident in our lives. Paul is adamant –

> *Walk in the Spirit and you will not fulfil the lust of the flesh* (Ga 5:16).

THE FLESH STAYS WITH US

Many people find it difficult to understand how "the lust of the flesh" can remain with them after conversion; yet it is true that all of us are still subject in one way or another to these fleshly traits. Conversion and baptism do not automatically eradicate from us all tendency to sin. In fact, becoming a Christian opens up for some people new vistas of temptation! Why is this so?

By the new birth and baptism we certainly become identified with Christ in his death, burial and resurrection. But this is basically a legal identification. It means simply that through faith in Christ we gain a legal right to all the blessings of salvation. But this legal right remains largely ineffective until it is realised and acted on.

Paul expresses it this way –

> *You however are controlled, not by the sinful nature but by the Spirit, if the Spirit of God lives in you. And if anyone does not have the Spirit of Christ, he does not belong to Christ. But if Christ is in you, your body is dead because of sin, yet your spirit is alive because of righteousness* (Ro 8:9-10).

Now that passage declares that spiritual life has come to us by Christ; we have been born of the Spirit, and to that extent the Holy Spirit dwells in us. But although because of the righteousness of Christ spiritual life has come to us, our "mortal bodies are still dead because of sin." Sin may still ravage our flesh though life has come to our souls.

But Paul does not stop there – it would be a tragedy if he did!

Rather, he goes on to affirm that if we, having been born of the Spirit and quickened spiritually, are then baptised in the Spirit, we shall also be quickened physically. So he says in the next verse –

> *And if the Spirit of him who raised Jesus from the dead is living in you, he who raised Christ from the dead will also give life to your mortal bodies through his Spirit, who lives in you* (vs 11).

So we find it needful, if we would express the fullness of God and the victory of Christ in our day by day living, to be baptised in the Holy Spirit.

But even should we be indwelt by the Spirit of God, we shall still find ourselves subject to, and bound by, the lust of the flesh unless we also **_walk_** in the Spirit.

So, after declaring the fact that God will "give life to your mortal bodies through his Spirit who lives in you", Paul qualified this remark by urging his readers to live by the Spirit –

> *Therefore, brothers, we have an obligation – but it is not to the sinful nature, to live according to it. For if you live according to the sinful nature, you will die; but if by the Spirit you put to death the misdeeds of the body, you will live, because those who are led by the Spirit of God are sons of God* (vs. 12-14).

Many Spirit-filled Christians who are not yet allowing the Holy Spirit to lead them, who are not really walking in the Spirit, have never experienced the wealth, the privileges, the authority, the revelation, the strength, the satisfaction, that only the practising sons of God can know.

This brings us to the question:

A) HOW TO WALK IN THE SPIRIT

1) Walk in love

See Ga 5:13-16. The first mark of the Spirit-led life is love.

We are not to strive with each other, but to love each other – by this we, and the whole world, will know that Christ controls us. In fact, the entire nine-fold fruit of the Spirit may be summed up in the one word *LOVE* –

- JOY IS LOVE REWARDED.
- PEACE IS LOVE AT REST.
- PATIENCE IS LOVE ON TRIAL.
- KINDNESS IS LOVE IN MERCY.
- GOODNESS IS LOVE IN DISCIPLINE.
- FAITHFULNESS IS LOVE IN CONFLICT.

- GENTLENESS IS LOVE IN SYMPATHY.
- SELF-CONTROL IS LOVE CONTROLLING.

Matthew Henry said –

> Christian churches cannot be ruined but by their own hands; but if Christians, who should be helps to one another, and a joy to one another, be as brute beasts, biting and devouring each other, what can be expected but that the God of love should deny his grace to them, and the Spirit of love should depart from them, and that the evil spirit, who seeks the destruction of all, should prevail?[39]

2) Walk in faith

a) The foundation for a successful walk in the Spirit is an unwavering confidence in the abiding presence of the Spirit, a deep assurance that your body is his habitation, and that he will not leave the temple that is his. Having once received the anointing of God, that anointing abides (1 Jn 2:27), and you should trustfully, joyfully, consciously, and continuously draw on the full power-potential inherent in that anointing. The admonition of Paul to Timothy is always apposite: **'fan into flame the gift of God, which is in you!'** (2 Ti 1:6).

b) Faith though, can flourish only in a certain climate. It is a delicate plant and soon wilts in a desert! For faith to prosper you must

First, apply yourself to every means used by the Spirit of God to produce Christian character; that is, Scripture, prayer, worship, fellowship with the people of God, and so on.

Second, in everything yield instant obedience to the Spirit when his commands reach you through Scripture, the preaching of

---

39) Matthew Henry's Commentary.

the Word, the proper exercise of spiritual gifts, the advice or admonition of mature people.

Third, have a greater care for your soul than for your body, love heaven more than earth, seek the favour of God more than the praise of men.

c) Do not permit emotion to be the arbiter of God's presence in your life. It is not important whether or not you can feel the presence of God, or feel strong in the Lord. It is enough that, having been baptised in the Holy Spirit you should believe in what God has given you. You must accept the declaration of Scripture that the fullness of the Spirit is not given and taken, but remains steadily with you. At any time you may lay hold of this incredible resource; in any time of need or trial you may claim the support and strength of the indwelling Spirit.

d) In this regard the singular evidence of the baptism of the Holy Spirit, speaking in other tongues, is of great value. Peter knew that Cornelius had received the gift of the Holy Spirit when he heard him "speak with tongues and magnify God" (Ac 10:44-48). So it is with us. In time of great need, when the grace and help of the Holy Spirit seem far removed from us, we can kneel before God, and with our hearts filling with love and faith toward God magnify the Father in the supernatural language of the Spirit.

To do this is to renew our consciousness of the abiding anointing, so that we may rise and boldly claim the might of the Holy Spirit in every conflict against evil.

It was for this reason that Paul, who said, **'I thank my God I speak with tongues more than you all'**, also said, **'I wish you all spoke with tongues.'** And, **'those who speak in an unknown tongue edify (or build up) themselves'** (1 Co 14: 4, 5, 18).

But note: it is your faith in the operation of God that will make you victorious. Merely to speak in tongues has no value unless you boldly claim the promise of God. Speaking in tongues is simply the outward evidence of the indwelling Spirit. As you speak in tongues you must allow the witness to rise in your heart that the mighty Spirit of God is resting upon you. You must arise from prayer deeply assured, and walk on, knowing that you are in-dwelt by the power of God.

Resist the devil. Resist the onslaught of evil. Yield to the guidance and persuasion of the Lord, knowing that the Holy Spirit will surely direct you in the way you ought to go. Then you will be victorious over all the works of the flesh.

e) To do these two things – to walk in love toward the other, and to war against the flesh by walking in the Spirit – will produce in your life the nine-fold fruit of the Spirit. As with Aaron's rod that budded overnight, so, the moment you begin to walk in the Spirit, the fruit of the Spirit will show itself; and as you continue to walk, that fruit will increase in abundance and beauty, until every work of the flesh is entirely subdued.

B) THE PROMISE OF GOD

Two great promises are given to those who walk in the Spirit:

First, 'against such there is no law' (Ga 5:23 NKJV)

That is, they will be dead to sin (which stands only because of the law), and triumphant over the works of the flesh. They will also stand pure and justified before God. Those whose lives are dominated by the works of the flesh cannot inherit the kingdom of God.

But the person whose life is dominated by the fruit of the Spirit, even though some failure and weaknesses may be found, will be free before God.

There is no law connected with the fruit of the Spirit, because there is no need for law – these lovely graces are their own law, entirely righteous and acceptable. There is no law, and therefore Christians whose lives are characterised by this fruit are free of any barrier between them and God: they have free access into the presence of God and stand high in the favour of God. The Lord has no restraint in his dealings with them. Because they are made full of fidelity and faith by that blessed fruit, he is able to heap on them his abundant blessings and every spiritual gift, and they will truly have power and authority in Christ.

Second, 'those who are Christ's have crucified the flesh with the affections and lusts" (Ga 5:24 KJV)

Those who produce the fruit of the Spirit will have in their hands the mightiest weapon for righteousness they could ever hold. As the works of the flesh are poison to the influence of the Spirit; so the fruit of the Spirit is the most deadly poison to the works of the flesh.

And also to the **'affections'** of the flesh. What are these **'affections'**?

The Greek word means **'hardship ... pain ... suffering ... influence'**. If these things are 'crucified' in us because we are Christ's, and because we are 'walking in the Spirit', then Paul is saying that the fruit of the Spirit is the fountain of victory over sin, sickness, failure, infirmity, and every satanic influence.

Now let the apostle bring it all to a conclusion (Ga 5:25; 6:9, 14,18 NKJV) –

> *If we live in the Spirit* (that is, if we have been born again by the Spirit, and baptised in the Spirit) *let us also walk in the Spirit ... And let us not grow weary while doing good; for in due season we shall reap, if we do not lose heart ... But God forbid that I should boast, except in the cross of our Lord Jesus Christ, by whom the world has been crucified to me and I to the world ... Brethren, the grace of our Lord Jesus Christ be with your Spirit. Amen.*

To place an order for *Walking in the Spirit* or Alison Chant's other book *Divine Healing* contact:

Vision Publishing

www.visionpublishingservices.com

1-800-9-VISION

1115 D Street, Ramona, CA 92065

www.ingramcontent.com/pod-product-compliance
Lightning Source LLC
Chambersburg PA
CBHW062224080426
42734CB00010B/2016